COMING OF AGE IN WARTIME

PHYLLIS WILLMOTT

Coming of Age in Wartime

PETER OWEN · LONDON

ISBN 0 7206 0696 9

PETER OWEN PUBLISHERS
73 Kenway Road London SW5 0RE

First published 1988
© Phyllis Willmott 1988

Photoset in Great Britain by
Rowland Phototypesetting Ltd Bury St Edmunds Suffolk
and printed by St Edmundsbury Press Ltd
Bury St Edmunds Suffolk

*For my children
and
my grandchildren*

Contents

Acknowledgements

Carl Harrison, Archives and Local History Library,
London Borough of Lewisham; and Michael Levien
for invaluable editorial help.

P.M.W.

Introduction

It is more than forty years since the Second World War came to an end. When the war began, I was a rather naïve and immature girl of seventeen, although probably no more so than were most girls in those days. I lived at home with my parents and brothers in the house we shared with my grandparents, two cousins and, for a while, two young uncles.

My grandfather was one of thousands who escaped from the harshness of life as an agricultural labourer by leaving his Suffolk village in 1879 to join the Army. After he left the Army he became a policeman at Lee Green in south-east London. He married my grandmother, then an auburn-haired girl who lived opposite the police station, and they raised a family of nine boys. My father and mother, unable after their marriage to find anywhere else to live in the difficult period following the First World War, accepted the offer of two upstairs rooms and a scullery in the house in which my father and all his brothers had been born. It was meant to be a temporary arrangement, but that's not how things turned out.

As a result, I grew up surrounded not just by my parents and brothers, but also by uncles, cousins and grandparents. In spite of the effects of unemployment, overcrowding and other privations common in the inter-war years, my early childhood was a happy one spent under the protection of what seemed to me omnipotent and usually amiable adults and bound by familiar streets amongst friendly neighbours. Life became more complicated, and less satisfactory, after I moved on to a girls' grammar school and began to look at my family and early environment with a more critical eye. I found myself between two worlds, a situation which, alongside the complications of adolescence, became increasingly painful. At sixteen, having successfully matriculated, I was glad to leave school. After a year as a very junior assistant in an exclusive private library, where to my chagrin I

found the class gap between my family and my new upper-class
friends at work even wider than the one between home and school,
I moved to a new job in the City. Three months later the war
began.

It lasted six years, so that by the time it ended I had, in more ways
than one, 'come of age'. Nowadays young people seem to grow up
much earlier, and many launch out on their own and have plans to
leave home and live apart from their parents almost before leaving
school. Had there been no war, my parents would have expected me
to continue to live at home until I got married and although, like most
young people, I was frequently resentful about the constraints that
living at home imposed, I am not at all sure I should have had the
courage to go off to live independently before marrying, had the
events of the war not plucked me out. This is just one of the many
social changes which have taken place in British society since the war
(and in some cases because of it), and which make the 1980s seem
such a different world from that of the thirties, forties and fifties –
especially to those who, like myself, lived through them.

Before, during and indeed for some years after the war life for most
people was Spartan by modern standards. Washing-machines and
refrigerators were still uncommon. Everyone in Britain – including
the middle classes – considered heated bedrooms were unnecessary, if
not unhealthy (except in the case of illness), and central heating in
homes was almost unheard of. There was no television, but listening
to the BBC on the wireless was an important part of daily life, as were
frequent (for many, at least weekly) visits to the cinema. The homes of
middle-class people were spacious and comfortable; such people
usually had telephones and sometimes cars. Those closer to the
bottom of the social scale, like me and my family, were more likely
to live in overcrowded and poorly furnished homes which lacked
not only luxuries but basic amenities such as electric lighting, hot
water and inside lavatories. In the outside world there were no self-
service stores, supermarkets or convenience foods. Local shops were
used daily by 'ordinary' housewives like my mother, with a
visit to the nearest corner shop for last-minute buys, and a once- or
twice-weekly visit to the street markets farther away, which were
reached by bus or tram. In the years between the wars, most women
stopped working outside the home as soon as they married and
turned their energies to keeping house. This pattern, as well as the
absence of refrigerators and frozen food, made the kind of cooking

women did and the food we ate quite different from what they are today.

My mother, like many others, stuck to a regular routine. She was thinking at breakfast-time what she would give us for the evening meal, and was off to the shops early to buy what she needed. Nevertheless, there was not much variety from one week to the next, because she worked roughly to a fixed range of menus. Cold meat and bubble and squeak, our wash-day supper, was a meal I hated, perhaps because it was served up so often by a tired and irritable woman. The rest of Sunday's joint, served up as shepherd's pie, was not much more to my taste because frequently it included bits of gristle that Mum had economically put through the mincer. Except for these meals (what Mrs Beeton calls 'cold meat cookery') the week's menus depended on cheaper cuts of meat. Most needed the slow cooking that housewives who were at home all day could attend to between other household chores. Toad-in-the-hole, stewed rabbit, stuffed hearts and stewed scrag-end of lamb were standard fare, always in my home served up on the plate with boiled or mashed potatoes, together with greens or carrots or parsnips or butter beans or tinned peas. Occasionally, as something of a treat, we had steak and kidney pudding or pie. Every day there was a substantial pudding to follow – stewed fruit with tapioca or rice, baked jam roll, spotted Dick or some other boiled suet pudding. Although rationing and food shortages brought changes, my mother's cooking remained much the same, but for many other women the war must have marked the end of this style of traditional English fare.

When the war began most people wore hats out of doors. For men, depending on their class or occupation, it was trilbys, bowlers or caps; in the summer panamas were not uncommon. Winter or summer, most men raised their hats when they met a woman they knew in the street, just as many gave up their seats to women on public transport. Women's hats, of course, were far more varied than men's, although soft felts were everyday wear in winter and straws in summer. Hats were an important part of a woman's wardrobe, and retrimming them was a pleasant pastime, as common as knitting. I remember one hat of my own of which I was particularly proud. It was a soft, rust-coloured felt with a small brim and a high squashy crown in a Tyrolean style. I decided to make it more striking by tucking a long pheasant tail-feather (bought at the local draper's) into the petersham ribbon round the crown, but this caused so many embarrassing stares – even whistles – that I shortened it!

Although the wearing of hats was so common, by the late 1930s it had become acceptable for young women, as well as young men, to go bareheaded in summer (in winter, headwear was generally thought to be a necessary precaution against catching colds). At the time older women, including the middle aged, virtually never went out hatless. On the annual outing to the seaside my mother and her friends from the mothers' meeting all wore hats – even on the beach. Gradually scarves and turbans began to take over. During the war women found that in the struggle to meet family obligations as well as keeping up the long working hours the war effort demanded, scarves and turbans could be used not only to tuck hair out of the way of factory machines, but to conceal hair in a mess – or a head full of curlers. Except for those in uniform, the obligation to wear hats petered out.

Before the war few women in this country wore trousers, then called slacks, although the more fashionable, influenced by Hollywood film stars, might have a pair to wear about the house or in the garden or for camping. I think my battledress issue on becoming an air-raid warden was my first experience of trousers, and that it was the Blitz which converted many other women to wearing them: for one thing, they could be hastily pulled on over night-clothes for treks to the air-raid shelter. In the women's services battledress top and trousers were standard issue, and many quickly grew to prefer them – as I did – to tunic and skirt. Trousers also found favour with the women who went to work in factories or who took over other jobs which, between the wars, were considered to be men's preserve. Lasting far longer than stockings, trousers became increasingly popular as clothes rationing made the replenishing of wardrobes more difficult.

The pre-war world was one in which class differences were still apparent in manners and style of life. Domestic servants still worked long hours for low pay, while families on more modest incomes usually had a charwoman. Middle-class housewives could run up monthly accounts at local stores and get most of their shopping delivered daily – quite often by errand-boys who had left school at the age of fourteen and rode round on bicycles carrying provisions in deep wicker baskets set over a low front wheel. Saturday jobs of this kind were also a common source of earnings for working-class boys before they left school. The war changed all that. Very soon, domestic servants vanished into the factories which were working flat-out on war production. As for the errand-boys, food rationing and shortages soon made their job unnecessary, and they were more likely to be riding their bikes around the district – as my young brother did – as ARP messengers attached to the local wardens' post.

Strangely, one thing that the war did not change a great deal was leisure pursuits. When the war began (and later on in the Blitz) people at first stayed inside their homes in the evenings. But it was not long before – behind the black-out curtains – pubs were again brightly lit and noisy, and cinemas crowded. Theatres, at first closed down, soon reopened and played to packed houses, often even when bombs were falling and the actors could hardly be heard above the noise of anti-aircraft guns. Slogans like *Is your journey really necessary?* helped the Government to encourage holidays at home. The aim was to relieve pressure on the overstretched railways. Holidays abroad were of course no longer possible, but package holidays as we know them today had in any case barely existed in pre-war days, and before jet flights had shrunk the size of the globe. A journey in the Golden Arrow to the Continent or a fortnight in Switzerland was the usual limit of trips 'abroad' (a word which had a far more romantic connotation then). Apart from the rich, foreign travel was enjoyed only by the more fortunate workers – professionals and those in white-collar jobs. For most people, if they had holidays at all, it was more likely to be a few days in bed-and-breakfast accommodation or at a primitive holiday camp.

Attitudes to work and authority have, like so much else, changed in the years since I left school to go to work. There was not the shortage of jobs for young people that there is in the 1980s. But getting what was considered to be a good job was not something that could be taken for granted. As a grammar-school girl who had stayed on at school until the age of sixteen (at a time when compulsory education ended at fourteen), I was considered to be amongst the more fortunate ones equipped for the better jobs available to the young. Amongst these, office jobs in the City were highly rated. The fact that to a young person this might seem boring or useless work (as it did to me), had to be disregarded. Security and relatively favourable conditions were paramount.

It was still very much the employer who called the tune and the employee who danced the appropriate steps. Routines and rules of behaviour were rigidly laid down and strictly enforced. One had to conform and do what one was told, always under the fear of getting the sack if one did not. At best, the rules were paternalistic, at worst dictatorial. This did not seem other than the natural order, and it was accepted as such by most people. Punctuality is one example. There was no question of getting away with arriving as little as five minutes late without some exceptionally good excuse; and the fifteen-minute coffee- or tea-break, or the hour for lunch, meant exactly that, and not a minute more. Similarly, offices and shops opened their doors to customers with unwavering punctuality. The underlying belief was that, in return for the privilege of working, employers had a right to expect loyal and dutiful service from every employee.

There were many other differences between 'then' and 'now', but the examples I have given show something of how much the world has changed. It may seem that the comparatively austere style of life which most people once had was hardly worth going to war to preserve. Yet few doubted that it was worth fighting for, with all its hardships and austerity. It is not, I think, too fanciful to suggest that, at least in part, it may have been the habits of this simpler, harsher and more disciplined pre-war life that helped Britain to hold on and win through.

This book is only coincidentally about that wartime period of history and how it changed my own life, as it did the lives of so many others. It is just as much about a stage in personal history which, in any age, remains recognizably the same. For all of us there is conflict between the need for stability and the need for change, and this is never more evident than in the years of approaching adulthood. It is the time when the long period during which the child has been dependent on home and family is coming to an end; the time of loosening ties and trying to let go. It just happened that, for me, this process coincided with the dramatic six years of the Second World War.

1
Summer 1939

It was Monday, 19 June 1939. Mum had called me a little earlier than usual with my early morning cup of tea. We knew I had to be in good time that morning because it was the day I was starting in my new job in the City. After Mum had given me breakfast and fussed round making sure I had everything I needed, I left the house and made my way through the park to the station, caught a train to London Bridge and had plenty of time to enjoy the walk over the river. My destination was the National Provincial Bank in Bishopsgate, an imposing building looking out on the junction of Bishopsgate, Gracechurch Street and Threadneedle Street. Two steps up from the pavement, through the lofty porchway and great double doors, and there I was nervously entering the immense banking hall, with its ornately decorated ceiling and high glass dome in the centre.

On this first day I arrived promptly at 9.15 a.m., the time I had been told to do so, which was a quarter of an hour later than the normal hour I should, like everyone else, have to keep from then on. I hesitated a second just inside the great door until I saw what I was looking for: the book on the high, open counter of solid polished mahogany that all staff had to sign every day, giving their time of arrival. Behind the counter, which ran almost the length of the hall, the long line of cashiers in sober suits, shirts and ties were busily counting and sorting out their piles of loose cash and generally getting ready for the day's business. As I reached the counter the nearest cashier looked across at me quizzically. Before I had time to speak, he said in a tone of voice that was somehow both fatherly and flattering, 'Yes, young lady, that is where you sign', and he stretched an arm across the wide counter to show me exactly where.

Following his directions, I found myself climbing dark and

17

gloomy stairs at the back of the banking hall, which led to an
equally gloomy room where the daylight was diffused from
windows too high to see out of. Although it looked like a
Victorian schoolroom, the clatter of noise there was more like
that of a factory. As I stood in the doorway I was overcome for a
fleeting moment by an urge to turn round and make my escape.
Even if I had dared, there would not have been time before a
short, rather round-shouldered woman with brown hair and
brown-rimmed spectacles extricated herself from between the
desks and came over to me. She introduced herself as Miss
Burns, took me across the room to an unoccupied desk and
proposed that I should make myself comfortable. I sat down on
the backless stool provided and tried to make sense of the scene
round me.

The clatter I heard was made by the half-dozen young
women already at work on what at my first frightened glance
looked like unusually large and cumbersome typewriters but
were, as I soon found out, ledger machines. How to work these
machines was, I now realized, what I was there for. I was
dismayed, because although at the interview for the job I had
formed no clear idea of what I should be doing, it had sounded
as if a rather more interesting fate was in store for me. 'Are you
willing to learn the skills you will need as a ledger clerk, and be
willing to do any work we ask?' had, for me, suggested a far
different prospect from that which this gloomy, noisy room
seemed to threaten.

But now that I was here, there was little I could do except
conceal my chagrin and follow the instructions that Miss Burns
was giving as she went round from desk to desk in the class.
From her first few minutes with me I realized I was not the only
person that morning to be disappointed. Miss Burns made it
clear how disconcerted she was to find that hitherto I had never
been in close contact with even the most ordinary kind of
typewriter, let alone this far more complicated equipment she
was expected to train girls to use in the brief time of two weeks.

As the day wore on I felt more and more cheated and
miserable, but I did my best to understand the confusing
instructions on how to tackle the monstrous machine in front
me. The day passed quickly enough, but by the end of it intense
concentration and the clattering noise sent me home with a

drumming headache and in a mood of panic and despair. Mum was sympathetic but made light of it; I would soon be as good as the others, she insisted. An early night, and it would all seem much better in the morning.

She was for once proved wrong. All night I was either dreaming or waking from dreams in which machines loomed over me threateningly and clattered endlessly. Before dawn I was awake again with an even worse headache, and when Mum came in to call me with my cup of tea at seven I burst into tears. After the aspirins she gave me made me sick, Mum reluctantly conceded that work that day was out of the question. 'You'd better stay here,' she said, not too good-humouredly, and then rushed out to catch my brother, Wal, before he left the house and to tell him he must phone my new employers on his way to his own job to say that I would not be in that day.

In spite of the bad start I had made, within a few days Miss Burns felt able to tell me that I was making good progress, and in just over the allotted fortnight I was ready to make my début in the banking hall below.

The National Provincial's head office, with its staff of hundreds, was huge. The building was linked by a spacious inner foyer which gave access to the upper floors, the basement, a quiet open space known as Fountain Court and to the bank's international department, which also had its own entrance in Broad Street. As is common in the City, the connecting way between the front entrance in Bishopsgate, the side entrance to Fountain Court (and the alleyway to which it led) and the entrance in Broad Street provided a useful passageway for many workers, as well as the clients and staff of the bank. This meant that from the time the main doors were opened to the public at 10 a.m., until their closure at 3 p.m., the cashiers behind their counter had a grandstand view on to a busy thoroughfare. And even from farther back in the banking hall one could, when standing, look out at the bustling scene.

Behind the cashiers at the open counter was a fairly high partition. It was not, however, too high for them to be able to consult with, or hand over things to, the supervisors, whose desks were spaced out along the inside of the partition and at right angles to it. The supervisors, of whom there were about eight, each had responsibility for a 'section' of customers' accounts; and along with this the responsibility for supervising the work of their three ledger clerks whose job it was to enter transactions on to customers' statements.

The ledger clerks and their machines were arranged in double ranks of three, all facing towards the long blank wall, and away from the counter, doubtless so that they would be relieved of any temptation to waste time looking at what was going on there. Beside each girl was a large ledger, set at seat-level, in which the bank statements were to be found in alphabetical name order. Twice a day each supervisor handed over to his girls the piles of cheques and orders whose amounts had to be entered on the individual statements. If any account became unexpectedly overdrawn – the machine signalled all overdrafts in red figures – it was necessary for the ledger clerk to draw it to the attention of the supervisor, in case he had overlooked something. At the end of the day the balance for each section had to agree to the last penny with the figure the supervisor produced. As each section worked as a team, between teams there was a friendly rivalry to finish first, and if a section's balance did not tally, a frenetic search ensued to find the mistake and put it right.

A successful ledger clerk was one who could combine high speed with accuracy. As a new girl I was placed in a section that had such a star performer: a young woman with blonde, bubbling curls and a high colour that suggested a country maid rather than a City clerk. Polly, whose diamond engagement ring sparkled as her pink fingers moved rapidly over the machine keyboards, was to be my tutor and guide. She was not only exceptionally fast and accurate but, luckily for me, extremely patient and good-tempered. When she had finished her own ledger, she would take some of mine. When I made a mistake, she would show me how to put things right, which could call for complicated manoeuvres of the machine. On days when my ledger failed to balance, she would forgo her lunch or stay behind at the end of the day until we had located the error and put it right. Probably like every new girl, I despaired of ever attaining the speed and accuracy that marked out Polly as much as her golden curls. But her imperturbable amiability was the best of incentives for me to try hard to improve, which I steadily did. Three months later I myself was given a new girl to teach.

In 1939 banking was a predominantly male profession and one in which, as I quickly realized, the prospects for women were virtually nil. Whereas the young men of my age were never taken on as ledger clerks and could expect to become supervisors, cashiers or managers in the fullness of time, for women the main road was to matrimony. Judging by the total absence of married women and the scarcity of older, unmarried ones, this was a destination which most women who strayed into the banking world reached soon enough. And indeed with so many young men around, head office at least served well as a marriage market.

In the banking hall there were regular lulls between the bursts of ledger activity, and during these there was time to argue and debate news headlines and exchange political views, or to discuss hobbies, holiday plans and stories, current reading and crossword clues. It was a familiar scene at such times to see one or two young ledger clerks, such as I was, leaning against the desk of their middle-aged supervisor and engaged in earnest conversation which had nothing to do with banking procedures. These interludes, however, were never allowed to hold up the flow of work. For one thing the supervisors seemed to be ingrained with what seemed to me an incomprehensible devotion to their duties. And for the ledger clerks there was always Miss Challis. Hovering not far away, she would swoop down on anyone guilty of too much chattering, especially if voices or laughter threatened to ruffle the dignified behaviour that she considered it part of her job to maintain. Aged about forty, bespectacled and bustling, Miss Challis was the 'lady supervisor' responsible for the female staff. As a former ledger clerk she was well qualified to judge who should go where, or to help out on sections whose work would not balance. She took care of those affected by headaches or female 'indispositions', taking them down to the windowless basement rest-room set aside for such occasions. She also kept a close eye on the appearance of female staff, making sure that none of them sat down at her desk without the issue navy blue coat overall not only on, but neatly buttoned up. She would not hesitate to suggest that a visit to the washroom was called for if hair became untidy or stockings twisted. And often in the mornings she was to be found waiting near the main entrance to see that the ledger clerks were wearing suitably appropriate clothes, which meant nothing too fashionable or at all unconventional. She was a kindly woman, if a bit of a fusspot, and amongst ourselves we called her 'Auntie'. She would sometimes gather one or two newer girls round her in a quiet moment for a brief pep-talk, and never missed an opportunity to impress on us our good fortune in being there. Banking, she would assure us, was not merely an occupation but a *profession*. The National Provincial Bank, as she proudly explained it, was amongst the most eminent in the banking world, and one of Britain's 'big five'. Auntie saw herself as a model of what the bank could offer to a woman prepared to give it lifetime commitment and loyalty. But she did not convince us. We were too polite to say so, but we all knew that we had no desire to end up like her.

2

Living with the Black-out

That summer saw the end of Mr Chamberlain's hopes for peace. Under the looming threat of war a profusion of Civil Defence leaflets arrived, telling us what must be done – if war should come – about evacuation, air raids, poison gas and the blacking out of lights after dark. At the bank, there was much more bustle and work because of the upheaval the preparations for war inevitably meant for City businesses. At home as well as at work there was a pervasive feeling of tension and edgy activity, even though everyone was determinedly carrying on with their normal lives.

On Sunday morning, 3 September 1939, only a few minutes after Chamberlain's announcement over the wireless that we were now at war, the air-raid siren sounded. Dad, Mum, Wally and I were in our upstairs kitchen, not saying much but all thinking about the solemnity of the occasion. Mum was no doubt worrying more about what was to happen to her 'baby', my brother Joe, a fourteen-year-old who only the day before had been evacuated to some unknown destination in Kent. And Dad was probably wondering whether on this exceptional day he would have to forgo his Sunday morning visit to his local, the Duke of Edinburgh.

It was not the first time we had heard the eerie, up-and-down wail of the warning siren; there had been practice ones before, but this was the first time that it might be the real thing. Typically, Mum's first thought was for her handbag, and her second was to urge me to pick up mine as we prepared to hurry down to the shelter which Dad had put up at the bottom of the garden in the spot where Grandad normally grew his vegetables. As usual, Mum made her way out to the garden through the side door, Wally and I following. Dad, however, went into the downstairs kitchen to make sure that Gran and Grandad were on their way. As Mum, Wally and I went past outside their kitchen window we could hear Grandad shouting at Gran in his bellicose way to stop fiddling about and get going. And as Gran followed us down the narrow garden path she continued to protest in her quietly grumbling voice that she had things to do for the Sunday dinner. Holding her by the arm as he gently ushered her onwards, my orphaned cousin Peter, who had lived with Gran all his life (he was seventeen, my age), added his reassurances to Dad's on the need to go into the shelter even though it was probably a false alarm – which it proved to be.

It was the first of several warnings in the week that followed, all of which also proved to be false alarms. But because I imagined from what I had read in the papers of bombings in Barcelona and Warsaw that the sky would be black with planes and that every building round us would be flattened, I was terrified. I kept my fears to myself, but probably I was not the only one who was more afraid during that first week of the war than they ever were later. Preoccupied with controlling my own feelings of misery and panic as we sat huddled together during one early morning warning, I was suddenly brought out of myself by the noise Grandad and Mum were making. I had grown up well aware of the chronic ill-feeling that existed between Mum and Gran, the traditional mother and daughter-in-law conflict, exaggerated by their sharing the same house, which sometimes led to sharp words and much backbiting. But Mum and Grandad had always seemed to have a bond of mutual respect and affection, and got on well together, yet now here they were in the midst of a terrible quarrel.

How or why it started I never knew, nor was it clear what it was about. But a fierce explosion of embittered accusations was going on between them. First Dad tried to intervene, with a brusque aside to Mum to 'Shut up!', then Wal, bravely risking turning Mum's wrath on himself, tried to jolly them out of it by saying that they were making so much noise we would at least not hear any bombs. These efforts succeeded only in making the pitch of Mum's voice rise higher and Grandad's swearing worse. I began to cry, at first only to myself and then sobbing out loud, 'Stop it! Stop it!' For a moment Mum did stop, but only to say sharply to me, 'You keep out of it!' Then, as quickly as it had come, the quarrel subsided. Grandad mopped his weeping eyes with his red, spotted handkerchief and Mum wiped hers on her pinafore. No one apologized; no one explained. We all sat there, miserable and silent. Bombs or not, our familiar world seemed to be disintegrating round us.

It was certainly a world transformed. Now we carried gas masks over the shoulder along streets made strange by walls of sandbags and blacked-out windows, returning home to spend quiet evenings reading or listening to the wireless, and going to bed never sure whether we would have to get out of it to rush down the long garden to the Anderson shelter. Yet within weeks life had settled back to much the same pattern as had existed before war was declared. Mum and Grandad seemed to have forgotten their quarrel; and Mum and Gran were on rather better terms than usual because they were united in their anxiety about the effect of the war on the family. Mum's immediate concern was Joe's unhappiness at being away from home. And Gran shared her concern because my cousin Ken, Pete's fourteen-year-old brother, had also been evacuated.

For me, life in some ways got better. Although at first the black-out kept me in at nights more than I liked, my working day was shorter. The pressures on the banking world that the preparations for war had brought about were behind us, but in addition, as one of the precautionary measures, some of the staff were evacuated to the edge of London, and this meant a reorganization of work which in fact shortened our day at head office. To my great delight, I now found I was sometimes finished and on my way home by four o'clock.

In consultation with Mr Iliffe, the office manager, it was one of Auntie's responsibilities to move her lady clerks from one section to another in the banking hall, or to other parts of head office where their services were required. Sometimes a move would be precipitated when she observed too close a relationship developing between ledger clerks or between them and their supervisor. Holiday and sickness absence had also to be covered. Yet other moves, according to Auntie, were necessary in order to give us the widest possible experience of the banking world. Despite the upheavals and losing her 'ladies' who had been evacuated, which surely must have made her job more difficult in some ways, Auntie managed to see that, as a new girl, I was moved around here and there to see other parts of the bank's work.

For a few days I was sent below to work in the strong-rooms where the bonds, affidavits and shares were stored. I was impressed by the immensely thick, shining steel doors to the safes which weighed tons and yet could be rolled tight shut with the merest pressure from the tip of one finger. The strong-rooms were air-conditioned and the atmosphere surprisingly comfortable, but the work I had to do – carrying stocks and shares about – was very boring and I was glad to get back upstairs.

Another brief break from ledger work in the banking hall came when I was sent by Auntie to the chief cashier's office which was, by today's standards, amazingly insecure, being not much more than a partitioned space behind the main thoroughfare. The door, it is true, was kept locked, but as this was in the partition wall, it was hardly robust. The job of young clerks like myself was to do up the large parcels of new notes that were sent out each day to the bank's branches. Each parcel of around £50,000 to £100,000 of notes had to be tightly wrapped in thick brown paper and tied up with strong string whose knots and cross-over points were then sealed with red-hot wax.

It was the first time I had seen notes worth more than one pound. Notes worth five pounds or more were much larger, and made of a crisp and tough white paper that crackled when handled. They were inscribed in a large black copperplate script and very beautiful. With my own modest salary in mind, as I processed such vast amounts of cash, I had puzzling thoughts about the value of money and disparities of wealth. Had anyone been tempted to run off with the loot? I wondered. The chief cashier told the story of one unfortunate clerk who had tried and failed; and, patiently explaining why it was more difficult than it looked to get away with such a crime, advised me to concentrate on not burning my fingers with the hot sealing-wax.

Back once more in the banking hall, I had as my supervisor a stiff, uncommunicative man who had something wrong with one side of his face which twisted his mouth and gave him a strangely glaring expression. It never occurred to me to ask him about it, but as he was only in his early forties it seems quite likely that it was the result of a wound sustained in the First World War. He had the reputation of being irritable, but I found no difficulty working with him. Nor did one of my fellow ledger clerks, a new girl called Gloria, who was soon involved in a brief romance with him, although he was married. One day, while we were dawdling at his desk between the tides of work, I asked him about the foreigner who I had noticed spent a good deal of time wandering about everywhere but who seemed to have no obvious job. This led to a discussion with his colleague at the facing desk. Between them they told me that the man was from Siam, a person of importance – some believed a prince – who had come to the bank temporarily to learn about British banking.

A few days later, as I was working away at my ledger, I found the man standing beside me. To my great confusion, his questions suggested that he was more interested in me than in the work I was doing. This was the first of several visits, of which the main aim seemed to be that of making me laugh – and blush. He addressed me as 'M-ees Thirteen' – thirteen was the number of my desk – and I began to have the feeling that he was watching me, and even imagined one day that he was following me after I left work. A week later I knew I was right when he stopped me on my way to London Bridge Station. In the office I had realized he was a small man, but now that he was standing beside me I found just how small. He barely came up to my shoulder. I was uncomfortably conscious of the curious looks from those hurrying by. To see a small, moon-faced man with narrow, shining black eyes and a yellow skin engrossed in conversation with a deeply blushing, tall, slim girl was not a common sight in the City. In excellent English, with only the slightest of accents, he began by acknowledging the embarrassment his teasing had caused me in the banking hall. 'You know, M-ees Thirteen, I think I have been very rude to you these last few days. I must make you a peace offering. What is your best free day? We will go anywhere you like!' Taken aback by this new approach, I was uncertain what to do, and ended up mumbling vaguely that I did not think I could manage any day. Unabashed, it seemed, my admirer detained me for a minute or two longer with his familiar light banter and then, politely raising his navy blue trilby hat, said, 'Ah, well – so long! Sometime in the future, then.'

As I went on my way across the river, I quickly regretted my refusal. Here was someone completely different from anyone I had ever met. A person of substance who could tell me all sorts of things about that exotic world beyond my own which I so longed to learn. I need not have worried as the days went by – which I did – that I had missed my chance. After ignoring me at the office for a few days, 'Meester Siam' (as I now thought of him) renewed his attack by appearing at my desk, pushing a box of chocolates at me and saying, 'I believe I still owe you a peace offering. When is it to be?' Aware of the intense curiosity of those round me, I was once again speechless with embarrassment, but managed to nod vigorously to the question 'How about Saturday?' It was the quickest way of getting rid of him.

This scene was, of course, observed with fascination by my fellow workers. Uneasy, I asked Polly whether she thought it was all right to go out, as I had now agreed to do. Polly said I might as well, for if I did not, I might regret it. Gloria, however, took the opposite view. A distinguished visitor to the bank he may be, but in her eyes he was a foreigner and not even a white-skinned one. I decided I preferred Polly's advice, thinking privately how strange it was that Gloria could be so superior when she had no qualms, apparently, about going out with a married man – which I thought was terrible.

On the following Saturday morning, after I had finished work, I left the bank and walked along to the Royal Exchange where, as arranged, Mr Siam was waiting for me. With obvious glee he told me he had just managed to get two tickets for the London Palladium that evening. I was put out because I had told Mum I would be home by seven o'clock at the latest. I knew she would be nervous about my being in the centre of London after the black-out. But the temptation of going to see the famous 'Gang Show' was too much. I allowed myself to be persuaded that we should call in at a post office and send Mum a telegram telling her I would be home late. Having done so, I put her worries out of my mind.

The rest of the day proved to be for me a dizzy whirl of delights. My first visit to a news cinema was followed by my first to a tea dance (which was slightly marred by the fact that my dancing partner was so much smaller than I was) and then on to my first cocktail bar in Piccadilly. Kit (the English abbreviation of his first name, Kitat) seemed a little disconcerted when, as the white-coated waiter hovered over us, I asked for a lemonade and refused to have anything stronger. It was the first of many little tussles that we were to have because of what Kit called 'your damned lower-middle-class morality'. Far from being offended, I was pleased to be linked with at least one characteristic of the middle class!

It was dusk when we left Princes Bar and Kit hailed a taxi to take us to the restaurant, our next destination. For me, taxis epitomized the life of high society – and, again, this was my first experience of going in one. Over our meal at Gennaro's (where, at that time, the manager brought round a bunch of violets to pin on the dress of favoured females), I found out that Kit was twenty-seven years old, which seemed a very mature age indeed to me. I was impressed to learn that he had been sent to England at the age of thirteen, to go first to public school and then Oxford, but appalled to discover that this meant he had not seen his family in Siam since he had left home to be educated. I found it hard to understand, too, that despite this long gap he seemed wholly to accept that before long he would have to return to his country and bow to the wishes of whatever his family had in mind for his future. As I sat opposite this strange-looking man, I was entranced by his courtesy, bubbling good humour and exotic smell – a mixture of expensive scent, oriental spices and garlic.

This introduction to a London night life that I had barely known existed, was also the beginning of an unequal relationship between an eager and hopelessly naïve girl and a sophisticated man from a completely different class and culture. 'You have, my dear Phyllis,' said Kit one day, 'an erroneous impression of Siam. It is not a country of Siamese cats, Siamese twins, white elephants and harems.' To press the point home that it was, on the contrary, an ancient and highly civilized society, he told me that Siamese students were studying in France at the time of Louis XIV. I was impressed – and even more so when I learned that Kit's father had been Lord Chamberlain in the reign of the ex-King of Siam. It proved that, although the rumours at the bank of Kit's princely status were not true, he was certainly the friend and intimate of princes.

On another occasion he made clear how much attachment he felt for this distant land, and his family there, despite his long absence from both. Although Kit was soon telling me how much he loved me, and I was thrilled by the romance of it all, he never spoke of marriage – and I knew that he would not do so. His family in Siam had other plans for him. This did not, of course, stop Kit from doing his experienced best to seduce me, although I was still much too proper to give way to him, infatuated as I was. When outings to the theatre, the Café Royal, Maxim's and night-clubs began to pall, Kit with some difficulty persuaded me to visit the more intimate surroundings of his Kensington lodgings. But by then my feelings towards him were becoming ambivalent, and then the progress of the war itself conspired against our romance. As an alien, Kit was forced to register and later subjected to restrictions on his movements and, as the war news got worse, I began to feel less and less comfortable going around with 'an alien', which caused us to quarrel. Soon after, Kit was called home.

Many months later I had a letter from Kit. He seemed to have got over his anger with me as well as England for turning against him. Perhaps by then he was pining a little for us both.

3

Encroachments of War

Inevitably, Auntie was amongst those who had noticed Kit's attentions to me. After our first outing together Kit came over less often to speak to me at work, but it wasn't long before Auntie appeared at my side and announced that on the following Monday I was to be moved into 'bulk department'. It could have been just coincidence, but more probably Auntie felt that the relationship between the bank's rather special guest and a mere ledger clerk was a bad example to the others.

Bulk department was just as vast as the banking hall but had none of its airiness and Gothic splendour. The ceiling was low, the walls a nondescript cream, and the large windows along one side (which looked out on to Fountain Court) were half painted over so that there was no view through them even before black-out blinds were put up. At the end nearest the banking hall one could see and be seen by Mr Iliffe, whose office, known as 'the Box', was another partitioned area of panelled wood with windows in the top half. At the far end, close by the huge, high table at which clerks stood to do sorting, a much smaller cubicle provided a kind of sentry-box for Mr Hampton, the manager of 'bulk'.

Mr Hampton was a gigantic man who, apart from an occasional beaming smile, maintained a benevolent but distant manner with the staff, unless one of the twice-daily 'counts' did not balance. Then, like a great bear, he would loom up beside first one and then another of the figures working away furiously at the rows of adding-machines in search of the error. On such occasions the clatter of handles being turned and the spewing out of yard upon yard of paper from the machines produced a fury of activity beyond the normal bustle of busy periods. Everyone knew and accepted that until the mistake had been uncovered and corrected we were doomed to continue the search. Any discrepancy – even just one penny – had to be found and put right.

It had been easy enough to understand the point of the ledger work I had done in the banking hall, at the chief cashier's and even the safes. But in 'bulk' I never fully grasped what was going on. In 'bulk' no one had their own desk to work at, and we spent most of the day standing up sorting piles of dividend cheques at the high table, or entering figures and then turning the handles on the adding-machines. One good thing about 'bulk', however, was that although the work was uninteresting, it did not always call for total concentration and so left plenty of time for talking. Under the eye of Mr Hampton, work on 'the clearing' at the high table tended to be a time of quiet and concentrated activity. But once one was at the adding-machines on the other side of the room it was easy enough to carry on a conversation with one's neighbour while fingers, hand and eye got on with the work.

Although we never became close friends, I often found myself talking to Amy, a pretty woman with black, shiny hair cut short and set in immaculate horizontal waves. Amy had been at the bank for over ten years, was engaged to be married, and looked forward to her future as a suburban housewife. To me, this seemed the ultimate in dreariness that life could offer – a view that Amy would dismiss with good-humoured but slightly smug conviction as no more than adolescent flightiness. With her conventional attitudes towards marriage, I was surprised – and a little disconcerted – to find that Amy's views on sex were actually more advanced than mine. She had been engaged for two years, but though her marriage had to be deferred until everything was ready, sex did not – with the help of a Dutch cap fitted at a clandestine visit to a private birth-control clinic. As Amy was already over thirty, it seemed all the more baffling to me, despite my reservations about her future way of life, that she should be so unconcerned at her age at not yet being married.

One or two of the more patriotic or impulsive of the young men the bank employed joined up as soon as war broke out, but banking was soon designated as a 'reserved occupation' and many stayed on until they were called up. Very soon after my

arrival at the head office first one, then another, of the numerous young men whose job seemed to be to wander perpetually
between various parts of the vast establishment, managed to
cross my path and invite me to join them for tea or coffee. It was
flattering to be asked, but I had no illusions that I held any
special charm for these young men, but then of course I was
new and not unattractive. I had quickly realized that for most of
the young males this mild dating was a kind of game they
played to enliven office life. It was a game I was perfectly
willing to play too, in spite of the uncontrollable and
embarrassing blushes I suffered at every such approach.
Whether I accepted or not usually depended on the whim of the
moment. To me it was much the same as being asked for a
dance at a local hop – something one could accept or reject
without a qualm. I turned down one good-looking boy because
of his arrogant manner and bright red hair, but I am sure my
rejection was not responsible for his volunteering soon after for
the RAF and subsequent disappearance for training overseas.
When he came back on leave a year or so later he sought me out
again. I had completely forgotten about him, but was all the
more flattered that apparently I had made such a lasting
impression on him. By now he was a bewinged pilot officer, and
the glamour of his blue uniform was if anything enhanced by his
red hair and public-school manner. This time I was only too
pleased to accept his invitation.

Another suitor I at first rejected was a tall, slimly built boy of
eighteen with hair like fine gold wire, a long nose above full red
lips and a delicately pointed chin. He suffered the disadvantage
of seeming to be almost more embarrassed than I was when
he approached me. Undeterred, he came back again a day or
two later, and what won me over was the combination of
his diffidence and obstinancy. Within minutes of sitting
down opposite him at our rendezvous, a nearby Kardomah
café, I recognized a kindred spirit. At first he did most of the
talking. His name was Donald Faversham. He was the only
child of well-meaning parents of whom he was very fond
but whose conventional ways he despised. He father held a
fairly senior position in the Post Office and, wanting him
to follow a similarly safe and secure career, had insisted that
his son should go into banking. Needless to say, this parental

intransigence inspired immediate feelings of sympathy on my part.

It was a sympathy that quickly deepened as, with his grey eyes glittering with the bitterness of his disappointment, he went on to tell me of his own ambitions. First, he pushed across the table some drawings he had done recently, and I was a little shocked when I saw that they were of nude women (imaginary, it later became clear). At the same time I was thrilled at what struck me as being daringly unconventional behaviour, and I took a sip of tea by way of showing that I could accept it nonchalantly. The drawings, Don quickly explained, were simply evidence of his artistic bent. His real talent, he believed, was in writing. He had already written several short stories (which he wanted to show me some time if I was interested in seeing them – I nodded eagerly to make clear that indeed I was). He did not expect, he said, to be able to earn his living by that kind of writing; but what made him so fed up with his parents was that they would not even consider letting him try to make a career in journalism.

We lingered as long as we could over our pot of tea, but there seemed no end to what we could find to talk about. Don had to catch a train from Fenchurch Street to get to his home at Leigh-on-Sea, but decided he would walk across London Bridge with me and escort me to my station first. On the way we stopped to hang over the parapet and went on talking while we looked down on the cargo boats and wharfs along the river banks below, or up at the sky where silvered barrage balloons floated like tethered whales. Don told me about Sylvia, a kind of childhood sweetheart to whom he was still very attached and perhaps, he warned me, still loved. I told him about Ben (my first boy-friend) and Kit and a few others, and made it clear that with my ambivalent view on romance and marriage he had nothing to fear from me. We arranged there and then to meet again on Saturday. Don said he would get tickets for the theatre.

On the Saturday afternoon we sunbathed in Hyde Park, and in the evening we went to see *Rebecca* (Daphne du Maurier was a writer Don admired). I was delighted with what I felt to be a new kind of enlightened and modern relationship which promised, as I saw it, to be an equal and mutually satisfying friendship between like-minded people. But my notions of equality between male and female were shaky, for I seldom made more than a half-hearted offer to pay my share of the bills!

Male clerks worked alongside females in 'bulk', and in general the males engaged in this work were young. There was, however, one man who, although he did not qualify (by my standards) as 'young', spent most of his time in 'bulk'. Mr Elgin was unpopular. He seemed to be looked on with suspicion not only by male staff but by many of the women. Apparently unperturbed by his unpopularity and, for his age, relatively humble position, he seemed content to exude an air of detachment and aloofness. As he always wore brownish coloured suits, not the normal dark blues and greys, the difference between him and the other men was even more noticeable. It was rumoured that, although he was highly intelligent, he had been passed over for promotion because of his unacceptable political views. Worse still, when war began, it had emerged that he was a pacifist, giving rise to further gossip that he was either a coward or a traitor. I was intrigued by the sense of mystery he inspired, yet disturbed by his reputation, and even more by his occasional penetrating glance when our paths in 'bulk' crossed. I determined to do what others did and keep my distance from him.

One of the reasons for James Elgin's unpopularity amongst the men was no doubt his unusual good looks which, it was rumoured, seemed to cast a seductive spell over women who unwisely ignored the warnings against him. He was not particularly tall, but he had thick, dark blond hair, fine grey eyes and a fluffy moustache above soft, pink lips. He retained some of the vowel sounds of his native Yorkshire, which should have been reassuring (but had somehow come to be regarded as yet another sign of his failure to conform), and he was unmarried. Despite his dubious reputation, in my view this at least mitigated his right to try to seduce females if he so wished. It was extramarital attachments which were in my eyes immoral; yet I quickly learnt that romantic entanglements of this kind were as common in the City, if usually as ephemeral, as dandelions in early summer. Like everyone else, I was soon able to recognize the signs that betrayed such affairs. There were the lingering looks, the box of chocolates hurriedly hidden, the whispered exchanges. And then before long the symptoms heralding the break-up would appear – pained looks from the men, and sometimes tears from the women – because it was rare that both parties were wholly serious. The men were only too aware of the cost of becoming too deeply involved. Divorce spelt disaster not only for the comfortable family life in the suburbs, but for careers too; divorce was a black mark against promotion prospects. As for the young women, they had usually succumbed to a mixture of flattery and the minor bribery of chocolates and flowers and invitations to restaurants or the theatre, embellished by declarations of love and tales of unsympathetic wives. But because for most of them the objective was matrimony, they soon came to see that they were heading for a cul-de-sac. One way or another, while hearts were continually being broken, most were soon mended.

Towards the end of the year I got to know another girl who had joined 'bulk'. Averil was a statuesque blonde with a downy complexion who, although not much more than a year older than I, was already engaged to her childhood sweetheart. Her fiancé had been called up and then suddenly sent overseas to be trained for a commission in the RAMC. This had left Averil to face alone the anxiety of whether she might be pregnant. Eager as always for a new experience, I agreed to go with her to a local chemist's shop to get some pills as, she said, she was now several days late. I was far more nervous than she seemed to be when we entered the shop, but not too jittery to notice that this was no new experience to the chemist. As Averil moved closer to the counter to mumble her request, the chemist gave each of us a look that somehow combined a professional blankness with a plain, but unsurprised, curiosity. I concluded that Averil must be only one of many young women who came here on the same errand. But what was harder to understand was why a respectable chemist in the City should be willing to offer this dubious service at a time when abortifacients from whatever source were illegal.

Averil's fears were short-lived, and soon after we were planning to go away together on a hiking holiday in the Malvern Hills. It had to be hiking because on our earnings – of 35 shillings per week – bed and breakfast was all we could afford; and we would have to go in March, because being young employees an early spring holiday was the best we could hope for. Not that I minded; I was impatient to get away as soon as I could for what was to be the first real holiday in my life.

Wearing tweed skirts and jackets, with ankle socks over our stockings and carrying rucksacks, we caught the 9.45 a.m. train from Paddington Station to Malvern Link and set straight off for the hills, stopping only to try the famous waters from a public pump. The sun was warm and bright, the air as strong and cold as the water. We had an exhilarating picnic lunch of cheese rolls and fruit. Reaching West Malvern around five o'clock, we found a place for the night at a house on the edge of the town where bed and breakfast was provided by Miss Maddox, who not only sounded but looked like a character from Mrs Gaskell's *Cranford*: she was small and grey-haired, had several large moles on her face, and was sweetly welcoming. For five shillings a head, her bed and breakfast also included supper!

During the night the good weather vanished and next day we set off in the rain to make our way to Ledbury, across the hills. We got very wet, and lost for a while when the mists closed in; and then, having taken a quick look round Ledbury, we walked on along the road to Great Malvern. By this time we were not just wet but soaked. Our bedraggled appearance must have been off-putting because we were turned away from four places before we succeeded in finding beds for the night. The weather continued to get worse, and our depressed spirits with it. We decided next day to hike again over the hills and back to the warmly welcoming Miss Maddox.

In the morning we awoke to a world white with heavy snow, which was still falling; and while serving our breakfast Miss Maddox told us firmly that she thought we ought to go home. Subdued by the elements, we felt inclined to accept this advice – a feeling that was confirmed when it took us almost five minutes to dig our way into the telephone kiosk where we went to ring the station at Malvern Link to find out about times of trains. But when we got to the station and found the sun had returned, we changed our minds.

Up on the hills again we found the snowdrifts were three-foot deep, the paths icy and the winds so strong that we felt in danger of being blown away. There was nothing else to grip, so we held on to each other as, shouting above the wind and laughing, we struggled to reach the beacon on the summit. On the vast expanses of snow-covered slopes the sun threw long shadows of sky blue and rose pink. I was jubilant. It was as if we had escaped into a new world or discovered a new planet.

By the time we got back to the hostel, which we had found close to the station and already booked into that morning, our faces were badly chapped. So too, despite our stockings, were our legs and thighs. Undeterred, we were determined to make the most of what was left of the week. Having tidied ourselves up as best we could, and after smearing our faces with cold cream, that evening we met a couple of school friends of Averil's fiancé, who took us out to dinner at a nearby country inn. And next morning, with the help of a lift from a passing motorist – who stopped to ask 'Are you real hikers, or would you like a lift?' – we ended up at Worcester eating a lunch of rolls and butter by the banks of the Severn before catching our train back to London.

Back home, everyone was pleased to see me, as well as relieved. Mum had been against the whole idea of my 'going off like this on your own'. She had herself had to leave her Bedfordshire village to work in London when she was only a few months older than I was, and she could not understand that any girl might *like* to leave – even briefly – the safe, familiar surroundings of home. Naturally, I gave her an expurgated account of our adventures, which did not include our hitch-hike to Worcester. But really neither she nor Dad were very interested except in my safe return. For them, real life was what was happening around them at home in Lee Green, or, so far as the wider world went, in the events that might affect their life there.

One event that concerned us all of course was the progress of the war. By spring 1940 the unreal hope of a short war had faded. The Germans had invaded Norway and Denmark, and France was in danger. At home too the reality of being at war was pressing in. Buses and trains were no longer on time, and when they arrived were always full. This unpunctuality or congestion had a brighter side in that it had brought a new friendliness into the streets. To break up the tedium of waiting, strangers had begun to talk to each other.

For Mum, because her main contribution to the war effort was to keep her own family fed and fit, shopping was taking up more and more of her time and energy. She was always out and about early in the day, but she began to complain that now she had to 'get out before the streets were aired'. I realized that she was having a hard time, but as I was at work all day I did not consider it to be any concern of mine. I was impatient with her recitals of how she had rushed first to this shop and then that, and did little to conceal my boredom, which sometimes provoked angry outbursts at my lack of sympathy. I was more interested in how the war was steadily encroaching on the lives of some of my friends, and not just those I had got to know at the bank. I still spent a good deal of my time after work, and at weekends, going about with friends who lived locally, to dances, or the cinema or, at weekends, hiking in nearby parts of Kent. One girl I knew called Molly had recently been evacuated with her office to Harrogate, while Sally – one of the friends I still saw from my old grammar school – was, much to my envy, going to be sent abroad. It hardly seemed fair that Sally, who on leaving school had so willingly opted for the dull security of being a civil servant, should have this exciting chance to travel. I was even more envious when I saw the smart new wardrobe her mother was making for her, and later read in her letters of the marvellous time she was having in Algeria. It was almost as upsetting when another of my old school friends, Anita, came round and told me that she had taken the plunge and joined the WAAF. Her parents were furious, she said, but as she was over eighteen there was nothing they could do about it.

One of the first of my male friends to go into the services was Ben – my first-ever boy-friend – with whom I was still on good terms. He had volunteered at the outbreak of war and was already on active service as a wireless operator in a minesweeper in the dangerous North Sea. Anxious to do my bit, I had for months been trying to knit a pair of thick woollen socks for him, but without much success. Since his departure in the early weeks of the war other young men I knew had gone off into the services, reappearing soon after on brief leaves, not yet at ease in their stiff, rough new uniforms. At the bank, too, the same sort of thing was becoming increasingly common.

As spring gave way to early summer and the sense of impending danger grew, everyone found themselves caught up yet again in a pervasive atmosphere of strain and tension. Invited to Sunday lunch by Ben's patriotic and conservative parents in late May, I found them putting a typically brave front on their anxiety. There had been no news for a week from this teenage son they adored, but they knew he must now be in the thick of the battle raging in the Channel. When the phone rang in the early evening, and it proved to be Ben, all their normal decorous restraints exploded into a joyous round of kissing and hugging and dancing. A week later, on a Sunday afternoon out on the Kent downs with Don, I heard the distant boom of the guns firing in France. Then, lying back in the sun on a haystack, we watched in awed disbelief as fighter aircraft swooped and screamed above us under the perfect blue sky.

Two weeks on and we had a rare visit from one of Mum's relatives – her nephew (and my cousin) Tom. I had never met him before, but I had begun to write to him once I found he had been sent with the Army to France. On that Sunday in June as he sat in the kitchen talking to us, his blue eyes were feverishly bright. He had, he told us, spent forty-eight hours on the beach at Dunkirk and, reluctant to say more, looked as if he could still hardly believe that his ordeal was over. 'It was hell,' he said briefly, and with such desperation that we all fell silent. 'Well,' said Mum after a pause, 'there's only one thing we can do, and that's live for the day. That should be everybody's motto now.'

4

London in the Blitz

The events in Europe, culminating in the dramatic evacuation of the British Army from Dunkirk, brought the 'phoney war' to an end. Britain, Churchill warned us, was now standing alone and at best faced a long, hard war. More prohibitions and orders were announced; rationing of tea and butter began; more young men were called up; housewives were asked to sacrifice their pots and pans to provide aluminium to make more fighter aircraft, namely Spitfires and Hurricanes. A frightening new leaflet, entitled *If the Invader Comes*, came through the letter-box. It made Grandad search out his bayonets (he had more than one, relics of his days as a Guardsman in Victoria's reign) and put them ready for action above his bed. And increasingly, day and night, the wail of sirens shattered the air. The Blitz had begun.

Within days, as it seemed, the familiar pattern and routines both at home and at work were totally disrupted. By early September, like the rest of London, we were adjusting rapidly not only to the frequent but unpredictable wail of the air-raid sirens but to the noise of anti-aircraft guns, the whine of descending bombs and the thud of explosions as they hit the ground. Since I spent a large part of each twenty-four hours underground in the safes at the bank or in the Anderson shelter in the garden at home, there was no alternative for me but to follow Mum's advice and 'live for the day'.

Living as we did on the boundary between the edge of London and Kent we were hit forcibly by the threat of invasion. At Lee, as elsewhere, a new, embattled spirit emerged after Dunkirk. Wal and Pete joined the Local Defence Volunteers (soon after to become the Home Guard) and Grandad got down his bayonets and, under the lilac bushes in the garden, insisted on giving the 'boys' the benefit of his instruction on how to use them. Having come back in the summer from their country billets because they had turned fifteen and were therefore old enough to start work, Joe and Ken were anxious not to be left out and volunteered to be messengers in Civil Defence. As the weeks of the Blitz continued, I was recruited as an air-raid warden and took my turns on duty dressed in navy blue battledress and steel helmet, with its large white W at the front. As a builder Dad considered he had more than enough to do repairing the damage to homes that the Blitz was inflicting; and Mum continued as before to believe that her main concern was, and should be, looking after her husband and children, as well as doing what she could to help Gran and Grandad cope with rationing and the shopping problems, which were getting steadily worse.

Some days passed by in a blur of raids, but I was no longer afraid as I had been at the outbreak of war. As time went by, like almost everyone else, I began to take a more casual approach to the new style of life that had somehow become the normal one. Blitz or no Blitz, the pull of the pub soon overcame Dad's fears. If the siren went before closing-time, too bad – he would take his chance dodging the bombs or shrapnel from anti-aircraft shells as he came home down the road. Gran and Grandad as quickly decided that they would stay in their beds and risk almost anything rather than spend their nights huddled in the crowded gloom of the shelter at the bottom of the garden. 'At our age!' Gran would grumble, as if the night raids were a personal affront from Hitler. And when morning came and I left for work Mum no longer bothered to ask if I had remembered my hanky or umbrella but whether I was carrying my gas mask.

Although at first we all went down to the shelter when the warning went and sat there until the all-clear sounded, we soon learnt that sometimes absolutely nothing happened. So we began to stay in the house until there was some sign of activity – enemy aircraft overhead or guns blasting at them. If it turned out to be a very 'noisy' night, we might all end up for a while in the 'dug-out' (as Grandad always preferred to call it, thinking of earlier wars); but as soon as it grew quieter, the drift back to comfortable beds began. It was pretty cramped in the

Anderson with Gran, Grandad, Mum and Dad, plus five young people. There were only four bunks, so not all of us could lie down, and even sitting up on the bunks was not comfortable. One particularly bad night the action began before we were in bed and all of us except Dad (who was already up at the Duke) went down to the shelter. For what seemed hours we listened to the drone of bombers, the clatter of gunfire, the whistle of bombs and the ominous crump as they hit something and exploded. In spite of this racket, everyone except Joe and me – we had made ourselves comfortable in the two top bunks – had slipped back to the house during lulls between the waves of activity.

I was woken by the sound of a cock crowing in someone's garden on the other side of the Quaggy – the little stream that flowed along the bottom of our garden. Remembering with satisfaction that it was one of my Saturdays off, I pulled aside the curtain Mum had rigged up across the opening that served as both entrance and window to the Anderson. It was not yet fully light and my watch said it was six o'clock. I lay back happily with my hands under my head. My face was about two foot away from the highest point of the curved arch of corrugated iron above me, and as my eyes adjusted to the half-light I saw dangling down from it, and dropping fast towards me, a huge, hairy spider. My frightened yelp woke Joe, who in response to my pleas made a bleary-eyed but effective lunge at the intruder.

Back indoors the smell of frying bacon coming from the scullery cheered us as we sat down at the kitchen table and Joe jokingly recounted his rude awakening. 'Sleeping through *that* night, then screaming at a spider!' exclaimed Mum.

The nights disturbed by raids were followed by chaotic days. To get to work it was no longer a matter of hurrying round to Hither Green Station to catch the train to London Bridge that in peacetime could be relied upon to be never more than a minute late. Destruction and disruption caused by the night's raids meant finding a way to work as best one could. Instead of the ten-minute walk to the railway station, my day now more often began with a walk to the end of the road to join the long queue in the High Road waiting for buses. When they came, most often they were crammed full, but the few cars and more numerous lorries that went by pulled up to offer lifts. Bumping along in the back of a lorry, standing or sitting wherever one could, seemed a far more interesting start to the day than being packed tight in the train. Most lorries then were uncovered (with a canvas top slung over in inclement weather), so there was plenty of fresh air mixed with the cheery chatter and banter of fellow passengers, young and old, office workers and factory hands, men and women, bank clerks and cleaning ladies all swaying along together in classless unity.

A bang on the back of the driver's cabin would bring the lorry to a halt when anyone wanted to alight. Most lorries were making only local journeys. It often took two or three lifts to get to one's destination, and a recurrent topic of conversation was the best way, in those circumstances, of getting where one wanted to go. Like everyone, I was prepared to take any vehicle that was heading, however roughly, towards central London. The general aim was no longer to arrive at office or work-place punctually – in my case, on or before the dot of nine o'clock – but to get there, somehow, as soon as one could. By the end of the day, and despite daytime raids, services would usually be running again more or less normally. But when there were raids during the day one was always afraid of returning to a pile of rubble where home had been. And every day, going or coming, there was new damage to witness: houses down in one street; fires smouldering in another; windows shattered, shops gutted, churches burnt-out shells; and always exhausted firemen with bloodshot eyes in a tangle of hoses, ladders and vehicles, still struggling against the damage the raids had inflicted. Later, to help workers get to the City and West End, a regular boat service started from Greenwich Pier. I welcomed this as yet another new adventure, but it brought home to me more than anything what was happening to London. As the boat chugged through the familiar viscous waters of the Thames, the scenes of devastation were numbing. For what seemed like miles, buildings on both banks had toppled into ruins. Clouds of black smoke rose from the tops of gutted warehouses, while in others fires still raged. Submerged by the acrid fumes, the familiar smell of the river, with its hint of the sea, had vanished. It was hard to believe that what I was seeing could be real. Yet, with a lump in my throat and tears welling in my eyes, I knew that it was.

It was on a Saturday morning when I had gone off to work at the bank that one of the German aircraft got through to drop another stick of bombs on Lee. I arrived home to find Mum in a state of emotional exhaustion and Joe looking pale. Our local wardens' post was based in the church school that Dad, his brothers and we children had all attended. It was a single-storey, red-brick Victorian building two streets away from ours. That morning, while Joe was inside waiting to rush out on his bicycle to carry messages, if called on to do so, one of the bombs hit the school. As Joe told us later, everything went black, something heavy crashed by and knocked his foot, and then there was silence. For one awful moment he thought perhaps everyone else was dead. Not on duty at the time, but idling around on his bicycle nearby, was cousin Ken. He was approaching the school when he heard the crump of first one bomb, then a second. The third, literally before his eyes, hit the school. Like Joe inside the school, at that moment Ken thought everyone must have been killed as he peddled furiously up to the sagging building, from which dust was still rising, and joined others in trying to get into it.

The blast from the bomb had done damage to houses beyond the school playground and in the street next to ours, so that Mum had not only heard the explosion but felt the edge of the blast in her scullery upstairs. She rushed down and opened the front door, and within seconds heard from a neighbour that the school had been hit. Snatching her coat from the hook on the landing, and not waiting to take off her apron, she dashed up the road. Sobbing as she ran, she arrived at the school just as the dusty figures came out. For Joe and the others it was a miraculous escape. Joe was the only casualty – a falling fireplace had bruised his ankle. In that first year of the Blitz others were not so lucky: over 95,000 were killed or seriously injured, more than half of them in London. One of the casualties was Dr Pat.

I was young and full of life but, like many young women, a victim of moods as unpredictable as proverbial April weather. No one was more light-hearted and gay than I when I was out with my friends, but it was often a very different picture at home. Suddenly, my spirits would plummet and everything looked black and hopeless. At such times I was discontented with my life and most of the people in it, especially those at home, and longed to escape to the wonderful world I believed existed somewhere outside my own. It was the world I felt I ought to be part of, although my vague longings and ambitions for what I was after were hard to define. In fact the only way I could express this desire for the more exciting life I dreamt of was to say that I wanted to travel. Quite often my moods of discontent were prone to result in vague symptoms of ill health. Although I was very thin and a bit anaemic, there was nothing really wrong with me, as my rosy cheeks, dark, shining hair and bright eyes proclaimed well enough. Even so, I had only to announce a headache, or tiredness or complain of obscure pains somewhere or other, to have Mum looking anxious.

Once we had started work, Mum's old worry over what to do when her children needed medical care was over. Mum herself (because she was 'only' a housewife), and Dad (because he was self-employed) could still not afford to be ill; but as a young worker I had become one of the privileged covered by the far from universal national insurance scheme that existed then. The scheme entitled me to free medical care from doctors who had agreed to participate in the insurance 'panel'. As Wal had done when he left school, I had registered at the general practice that we had to pass each day on our way to work. It was very near Hither Green railway station, which was the one we used daily to get to the City. The practice belonged to two Irish brothers, Drs Edward and Patrick Carey, and it was in the family home of Dr Edward Carey, the eldest brother. It was a corner house of red brick, with the generous-sized bay windows of the more spacious suburban houses built around the turn of the century. The entrance to the surgery was at the side of the house and opened off the approach road to the station. The door of the surgery led straight into the waiting-room, and at the other end of it were two tiny consulting-rooms and, between them, a third even smaller one – no more than a cubicle – which served as the dispensary. Prescriptions were handed over by a severe-looking woman through a small hatch, which she would open when the prescription was ready. She would also peer out from it bad-temperedly when anyone rang her bell to make some inquiry. The waiting-room adjoined the family living-room in which one could sometimes hear the reassuring noises of Dr Edward's children laughing or quarrelling when they were at home in the holidays from boarding-school. It sounded a happy family life in there, but one that was hard to associate with the intimidating figure of Dr Edward (as we called him, to distinguish him from Dr Pat). Dr Edward was not exactly stern or severe or unfriendly, but his bustling and hurried manner was not the kind to put a nervous girl at ease. Having to see any doctor made me feel nervous, even though with Dr Edward I knew I should barely have time to say a word before he would be assuring me in his thick Irish accent that all would be well – a fair diagnosis, one might think, from the look of me. What I did not know then was that Edward was not only a conscientious doctor but a thoughtful and compassionate man of wide interests whose only relaxation was reading late into the night in rare, quiet moments during his long working hours. The war had made his work even harder and, not surprisingly, he no longer had the patience or energy to waste much time on girls like me. This did not help my uneasiness which, on the contrary, always had plenty of time to increase during the long wait in the bleak and dimly lit waiting-room. On top of this, it was not reassuring each time he appeared at his door to see that Dr Edward was looking gloomily along the rows of those still waiting as if already trying to assess what troubles there might still be in store for him.

On some occasions the hours of waiting were made even longer either because one of the doctors was held up on some emergency call outside or had been called away to one during the surgery sessions. It was on such a day that I found myself crossing the waiting-room to join the queue for Edward's brother, eventually entering Dr Pat's consulting-room. The room was just as small as Edward's – that is, not much more than a large cupboard – but in some unidentifiable way brighter.

Edward's habit when one went into his room was to instruct his patient to sit down but to remain standing himself. As the room was so small, he seemed to take up most of the space, with his stout, black-coated body too close to the patient and his face like a moon above. In Dr Pat's room I found myself not looking up but *down* on to a head of light-brown hair topping a pleasant, square-shaped face. Seated at his desk, Pat looked up at me quizzically. 'Sit y'down,' he said in his equally thick Irish accent – something he did have in common with Edward – before going on, 'Now don't hurry. Just tell me in y'r own way what's t'trouble.'

Before I knew it, I was telling him not only about the sore throat (which I hoped was going to provide the excuse for a day or two off work) but about my irregular periods that worried Mum but not me, the occasional spots on my face that worried me but not Mum; and then all about my job, my frustrations and my dreams for the future. He listened, sympathized and gave me the flattering impression that he cared. I don't suppose he spent much more time on me than his brother would have done, but it felt much longer, so that when I got up to go I had almost forgotten I was supposed to be ill. Knowing I had found a friend, I went home in high spirits.

From then, on the need to 'go round to the doctor's' became, for me, something to look forward to rather than dread. But not for long. Only two hundred yards away from the surgery the large marshalling yards of Hither Green Station were to prove a frequent target for Hitler's bombers. It was on one bad night that Dr Pat was caught on his way to a call and killed instantly.

As Christmas came nearer we all began to wonder what kind of a festive occasion it could possibly be this year. Would the Germans give us a break from the bombing, or would we be eating our Christmas pudding to the sound of sirens wailing, bombs falling, guns barking and shrapnel hitting the roofs? Wal and Pete were on Home Guard duty on Christmas Eve, but at the end of an evening without incidents they came clattering up the stairs in their heavy boots demanding 'cocoa for the boys'. With them was a new friend from their platoon who soon had us laughing loudly at his tales of disarray in this motley collection of part-time soldiers.

Andrew Cooper was four years older but only a couple of inches taller than I was. He had a thick mop of silky dark hair, which he would smooth back with his hand when it fell over his forehead. His mouth was wide and his lips very red; his blue eyes were expressive, changing according to his mood from sparkling, mischievous brightness to soft dreaminess. Mainly because of his colouring, but also a kind of gentleness in his manner, he had an almost feminine beauty. To the dismay of Wally, his new friend showed every sign of being as interested in me as I was in him, and refused to be put off by Wal's warnings on my unreliable behaviour towards admirers who had the misfortune to 'fall into her clutches'. Andrew lived with his parents in one of the newer houses that had sprung up during the 1930s round the edges of the older part of Lee which I had grown up in. His parents' house was a ten-minute walk away from mine. It was in a road that I knew well because one of my old grammar-school friends, with whom I had sometimes played a game of tennis in the park, also lived there (her brother, it turned out, was a friend of Andrew's). I was a bit disappointed to find that Andrew had not been to a grammar school. And although very well mannered, and almost genteel in his politeness, his south London accent sometimes jarred on my refined grammar-school ears.

One of the things that attracted me to Andrew was that he had the kind of artistic and intellectual qualities which I most admired and aspired to find, if not in myself then at least in my ideal lover. Andrew's talents were certainly promising. He was an amateur painter and witty cartoonist; he wrote stories and poetry (about which I knew very little); he played the piano, loved classical music and opera (about which I knew even less). These were the kind of attributes that were given scant respect by my family, but at the same time were seen by them to make Andrew an obviously suitable companion for me! Fortunately, Andrew had two other attributes that weighed far more in his favour with Mum and Dad – a highly respectable job as a draughtsman and a sense of humour.

About three months after our first meeting, on an evening when neither of us had to be on duty, Andrew and I decided to go across to Greenwich and have a long walk by the river. Before we returned home the siren had sounded and the anti-aircraft guns were firing away furiously. For a while we stood in the porch watching the searchlights criss-crossing and sweeping the dark sky, enjoying the noise of the barrage from the guns and listening to the sound of enemy aircraft overhead.

It seems a strange way of spending an evening, but to us at the time it was just part of the way of life to which we had adjusted. Before long Wally and Pete arrived back from Home Guard duty and joined us in the porch, from which on several occasions we had to make a dash back into the house when we heard the whizz of descending bombs. Seconds later we also heard crackling noises and Andrew exclaimed, 'Quick! It's incendiaries!' He and Wal each picked up a stirrup-pump, Pete grabbed sandbags, I took a bucket of water and we then raced down the front garden path and along the road. Incendiaries seemed to be everywhere, but so too were numerous fire-watchers like ourselves.

At the end of the road an agitated old lady with abundant snow-white hair called us into the almshouses where a room had caught fire. Hardly able to breathe or see because of the burning smoke, we managed to put out the fire, and from then on for over two hours we rushed hither and thither, putting out others. We climbed into lofts, tore away burning wood with bayonets, clambered through the broken window of the Methodist church, chased up and down stairs in the tall Victorian houses in the High Road, and everywhere humped along our stirrup-pumps and pails of water. It was past midnight before we were done. As the red glow in the sky told us, there were still plenty of fires raging, including one in the furniture depository nearby. We went along to see if there was anything we could do there; giant tongues of red and gold flames were shooting skywards from the glowing building and clearly this was not work for us. In any case the firemen had already arrived.

With blackened faces and clothes soaked we returned home, still carrying the precious pumps, sandbags and bucket. After Mum had made us all a cup of cocoa to warm us up, I walked to the end of the road once more to see Andrew on his way. With relief we saw that the angry red glare in the sky from the blaze of fires was lessening, suggesting that even the big fires were now under control. Next morning I could hardly get out of bed. Unused as I was to heavy physical work, now after an evening of hauling on sandbags and fetching and carrying full pails of water I felt stiff and bruised all over.

It was some weeks later that a bomb dropped and exploded

just round the corner in Brightfield Road. It was not a large bomb, but the crater extended across the road and burst the main gas pipes below it. It also wrecked or destroyed several houses on each side of the road, but miraculously no one was killed and only two were taken to hospital. The blast across the back gardens shattered windows over a much wider area and, as we were soon to find, damaged the structure of nearby houses, including our own. From then on, whenever Gran (or more often Grandad) lit the fire in their downstairs kitchen, ours upstairs quickly filled with smoke. Most of the smoke went away after a while, but every time it happened Mum got frantic about it, and angry with Gran and Grandad, even though she knew they could hardly be expected to give up having a fire when they needed one in the cold days of early spring. The bomb, Dad said, had cracked the chimney-breast, but it was not something, apparently, that he – or therefore, I suppose, anyone else – could easily put right. Before long, even Dad had to agree that there was nothing for it but to move out and that he would keep his eyes open for a suitable new home for us.

He did find one a couple of streets away. It was right next door to the church school in which Joe had been when it was hit by a bomb. The school was a ruin but, although the former tenants of the house had moved away after the bombing, it had suffered barely more than shattered windows and lost roof tiles because of the unpredictable vagaries of blast from the explosion. The battered school building was not an attractive sight, but what Dad liked particularly about this house was a large yard at the back, which was also available for renting. The blast from the bomb had done much more damage to some other houses which stood farther away from the school at the end of what had been the playground. The houses were derelict, in fact, which meant that, by clambering through the rubble, one could take a short-cut to our old house, almost within shouting distance. After sharing a house with his parents for over twenty years Dad had no intention of moving far away from them, especially in the midst of a war.

I was as thrilled as Mum at the prospect of our having a whole house of our own. For her it was a dream she had waited for since her married life had begun a year or two after the First World War ended; a dream that she had almost given up hope of ever coming true – and which may well not have done, had there been no war and no Blitz.

It was summer by the time we moved out of our old house, and by then the air raids had ceased for several weeks, which added to our sense of beginning a new life. That morning I went off to work in the ordinary way. I suppose because of the rush to get off to work, I did not even say goodbye to Gran and Grandad, but I am sure Mum did before she finally left the cramped upstairs rooms in which she had shed so many tears during those long, harsh inter-war years. Despite her joy at moving at last to a home of her own, free from her mother-in-law's insidious influence, I have no doubt her brown eyes were liquid with tears as she made some kind of awkward farewell. And I am equally sure that Gran was very angry as she watched Mum's three-piece suite being moved out of the front room – *her* front room, from which a few years earlier her own horsehair furniture had been thrown out to make room for a bed-settee for me to sleep on because I was too big to share Mum and Dad's bedroom any longer.

At any other time Mum would have made much of such a domestic drama, but on this day when I returned home from work she was much too busy getting things straight, telling me about what still had to be done and, despite her tiredness, delighting in the spaciousness of our new surroundings. It was the end house in a short terrace, and separated from the school by the entrance-way to the yard which ran along the side of the house and our small back garden. Our new home seemed very grand compared with the two rooms and a scullery we had lived in upstairs in Grandad's house. However, it had only gas lighting, not the electricity I had hoped for, and there was no bathroom. The lavatory was just outside the kitchen door, but enclosed by the conservatory that had been built on to the back wall of the house. Dad had already replaced the shattered glass in the conservatory, repapered some of the rooms, and was going to put in a bathroom as soon as he could.

There had been much discussion about which room I could have for my bedroom. I had a choice between a small room on the half-landing or the attic room, which Dad thought might appeal to me more because, since it had a sloping ceiling, it would make me feel like an artist in a garret. Whichever room I did not have, Dad would use for the bathroom. To his surprise, I decided to have the landing room – I was not quite so stupidly romantic as Dad believed, for I realized I might find the attic a bit too icy in winter and too hot in summer. I also liked the idea of having a fireplace, diminutive as it was, because I hoped (without much success, it turned out) that I might be able to persuade Mum to let me have a fire there when I wanted to be on my own.

I made a trip with Mum to The Times Furnishing Company in Lewisham where, as well as a dining-room suite, we were to buy a single bed for me (all on 'easy terms', of course). There was a narrow cupboard built in the small recess by the fireplace in my room that I could use as a wardrobe and, because she did not have to get one of these for me, Mum was willing to be indulgent when she caught me looking longingly at a small oak writing bureau. It had two shelves for books at the bottom and a small cupboard at the top with a door that could be dropped down to serve as a desk. I had persuaded Dad to paint the walls of my room in pale green, rather than have the wallpaper that he and Mum wanted. There was a half-moon-shaped green rug in front of the fireplace, and green lino the previous tenants had left behind, and I was very satisfied with the total effect, never mind that Dad said it looked more like a prison cell than a proper bedroom.

Now that Mum had not only her own front room (which, when we remembered, she and I sometimes called the sitting-room) but a living-room in which we ate our meals on a splendid new table and also spent most of our time, Mum and Dad were prepared to be far more hospitable to both their own friends and ours. Now, Andrew was always welcome for a cup of cocoa after Home Guard duty or when we came back together from dances, walks or the pub, and a frequent visitor for tea on Saturdays and Sundays.

5

Pluckie

I had been in bulk for more than a year when Auntie informed me that I was to return to the banking hall. This time I was to be on the section for foreign accounts, one for which only the more skilled ledger clerks were used. The supervisor, Mr Dallinger, a tall, large-boned man with slicked-down hair topping a long, lugubrious face, was one of the most committed and skilful of those addicted to the *Daily Telegraph* crossword. He had the reputation of being stern and uncommunicative, but his doleful expression concealed a tolerant and thoughtful man of wide knowledge, and I soon noticed that when his slate-blue eyes gleamed with sardonic humour, which they often did, he did not look stern at all.

The ledger clerk with whom I was to share the work of the foreign section was a young woman who looked liked a shy schoolgirl. She was half a head shorter than I was, with wavy brown hair, a rose petal skin, blue eyes and delicately pretty hands. Explaining the new section to me she spoke in a quiet, almost prim, tone of voice that unexpectedly combined humility with obstinate assurance. It struck me that the same kind of contrasts were reflected in her name. Her friends, she told me in that quietly contained voice of hers, usually called her by her school nickname, Pluckie, but her real name was Emily – Emily Pluck. At first sight I did not feel that this reserved little person was one with whom I should have much in common. But we were soon at ease with each other, the differences in our personalities not seeming to matter because of our appreciation of Mr Dallinger, especially his quiet sense of humour.

We settled to work together as a harmonious team, taking great pride in our speed and accuracy. In happy co-operation

with Mr Dallinger, who was himself extremely efficient, we
found we had plenty of time between the rushes of work to
huddle by his desk discussing crossword clues (and the fine
points of meaning, grammar or literature that these prompted).
We also enjoyed arguments about the day's news, during
which 'Mr D' would set his well-informed but mildly conservative views against our ignorant but vehemently radical
ones. From the grand heights of our innocent naïveté we
delighted in proclaiming 'advanced views' on contraception,
abortion, 'free love' and the unacceptability of marriage. We
were equally eager to expound our socialistic ideals, although
neither of us belonged to any party, along with our contempt
for capitalism and all its works (which naturally included
banking).

I found that Pluckie's ambitions for a future career outside
banking – and, with less certainty, outside marriage – were
much like mine although rather more realistic. Her main
ambition, she said, was to be a painter; but her practical plan
was to continue to educate herself in the hope that this might
somehow lead the way to a more satisfying job. As we ate our
sandwiches one sunny day in St Botolph's churchyard, Pluckie
told me about Morley College, where one could attend evening
courses of a university standard. It was on the other side of
Westminster Bridge. The autumn term would soon be starting
and it was there she proposed to begin putting her plans into
practice. I said it sounded interesting and perhaps I would go
with her.

In spite of the war and the Blitz we still found plenty of things
to do in our free time. In our lunch-hours we often went to piano
recitals in the City churches; and less frequently we walked
along to the Tower, where part of the outer wall had recently
been bombed, but speakers still ranted daily on Tower Hill.
One day we much enjoyed a Scotsman – he was either mad or
drunk – swearing and abusing Winston Churchill. On another
occasion we listened sympathetically to Sybil Thorndike plying
her beautiful stage voice in the cause of pacifism. During coffee-
and tea-breaks our serious (but by no means always earnest)
conversations continued, and the more we talked, the more
delighted we became with each other's company. Inevitably,
we enjoyed exchanging confidences about our admirers. I told

Pluckie about my more recent adventures: the exciting inter-
lude with Kit ('the Siamese gentleman!' she exclaimed incredu-
lously); my current friendship with Don – 'sort of platonic', I
explained; and my blooming romance with Andrew. Although
mildly disapproving of my careless and light-hearted attitude,
Pluckie contrived to excuse me on the grounds that I had been
flattered by too much attention and that it was therefore hard
for me not to be confused! Because of her own interest in
painting, and from what I told her about Andrew, Pluckie was
predisposed to consider him as a more promising suitor.

For my part, I was amazed to hear that Pluckie was on close
terms with that much talked about person, James Elgin. It was
clear that this enigmatic man had roused in Pluckie not hate
but an admiration bordering on idolatry. I found out that one of
the things which had drawn them together was a commitment
to pacifism. According to Pluckie, James Elgin was the most
intelligent man she had ever met. His knowledge spanned
politics, philosophy and literature, his thinking was profound.
In short, Pluckie admitted that she was his devoted disciple,
and I concluded – despite her protestations – that she was at
least half in love with him.

I began to see James Elgin in a more favourable light, and
now when our paths crossed in the bank I no longer avoided his
glance, aware that he knew of Pluckie's growing friendship with
me just as I knew of his with her. Talking one day about books,
I happened to tell Pluckie that I wanted to find a book of
Keats's poems for the small 'library' I was in the process of
collecting to fill the two shelves of my new bureau. Pluckie told
me she would ask James, who would be sure to know where I
could get a second-hand copy. A day or two later she came back
with a message that James would be pleased to take me to
bookshops he knew to find what I wanted. Pressing me to go,
Pluckie assured me that she did not mind; that even if she did,
she would have no right to; that she was not James Elgin's
'sweetheart', and not the only girl he knew and went out with.
This fitted in very well with my own ideas about friendships
with the opposite sex, so I arranged to meet James after work
one Saturday afternoon.

We got on a bus to the West End, and though I tried hard to
act as if I were completely at ease, I wasn't. I realized again that

there was something disturbing about this flaxen-haired man. It was more than his good looks, more than the sum of his cream-coloured skin, misty-grey eyes and the soft, bushy moustache above the well-shaped pink mouth below it. There was a kind of magnetism about him which was both attractive and repellent. What was I doing out with this man? I asked myself. Why had I agreed to meet him? Thinking of Pluckie's spellbound admiration for James, and then of Andrew's ill-concealed jealousy when he had heard about this outing, I blushed with guilt. I made up my mind to get away as soon as possible and avoid any further entanglements of this kind. But all my disquiet vanished as we wandered around bookshops together. It was so pleasant to be guided and advised by someone who seemed to know not only every back street in Bloomsbury, as James informed me this was, but exactly where to find any book.

For not much more than five shillings I became the owner of a *Chambers Dictionary*, a complete volume of Keats's works and a book on Dr Johnson. The book-buying done, James offered to take me for tea to a back-street café, where we lingered until he suggested we move on to continue talking in his room nearby. This room was almost as small as my own at home, but I was impressed by its view over tree-tops on to the British Museum. Sitting on James's divan (while he sat on his low, mauve-covered armchair opposite), I hugged my knees in delight at what still seemed to me this daringly unconventional act of being alone with a man in his bed-sitting room. But either convention or caution was not far below the surface! As the daylight showed signs of fading I left for home, proudly and conspicuously carrying the three solid volumes under my arm.

Avid for culture as we were, Pluckie and I were determined to benefit as much as we could, despite wartime controls and bombs, from what London had to offer budding intellectuals like us. It was almost a principle always to have a book under the arm – preferably one with the bright yellow cover of the Left Book Club (although I found these easier to carry around than to read). One had adjusted to black-out and Blitz, and so it was again part of life to go to concerts, theatre or ballet, and not at all unusual to find one's way home afterwards to the sound of anti-aircraft guns and falling shrapnel. It did seem odd to be walking from the station at Hither Green past the rows of ordinary little houses in such extraordinary conditions. Yet at the same time the very familiarity of these streets reassured me. With my warden's steel helmet tipped slightly forward, because what I most feared was a disfiguring wound to my face, I hurried along, anxious enough to get home as quickly as I could, but at the same time, with all the optimism of youth, unable to believe anything would happen to me. Fortunately, by the summer the Blitz seemed to be over, apart from sporadic raids.

It was early September 1941 when Pluckie reminded me that the autumn term at Morley College began that evening and that I had said I was going to enrol for the course on philosophy. I had completely forgotten about saying I should like to join her when Pluckie told me about her plans for self-education. When Pluckie told me she had arranged with her mother to give me tea before the evening class, I knew I had to go. From what I had heard of the uneasy relationship between Pluckie and her mother I realized that if I did not turn up it would go hard with Pluckie when she got home.

One of the benefits following our move, coupled with the importance that the Blitz had given to Dad's work as a builder, was that we now had a telephone in our house. I rang Mum and explained I would be late, which of course irritated her because she had used up rations for an evening meal she had prepared for me. 'You'll have to have it heated up for tomorrow,' she said crossly, which was just what Mrs Pluck would have said to Pluckie rather more forcibly, had I not turned up for tea as arranged.

Pluckie lived in north Lambeth, not far from Morley College. She was one of the few people at the bank, and certainly the only ledger clerk, who lived within walking distance. However bad the Blitz, she had never been late arriving, and indeed took pride in the fact that she, at least, was still maintaining the high standard of punctuality which had been expected of everyone until the Blitz put an end to it all.

On this occasion we did not walk but took a bus to Westminster and then walked across the bridge and the rest of the way through the sandbagged and rubble-strewn streets. Pluckie's home was in a faded terrace of small Georgian houses built in yellow brick around a small triangle of open space. It had a few plane trees at the edge but, like the houses, the 'square' had seen better days. In the middle of it the ugly black shape of a shelter for the residents further detracted from its remaining charms. But at this time of the day there was a brooding air of gentility lingering about the place, although Pluckie told me that when the men rolled home from the pubs at night it was very different.

We walked up the short flight of stone steps to the front door. It opened into a narrow passage, off which was Pluckie's room. It looked directly on to the square through a window that seemed large in proportion to the small, pleasant room. Pluckie's sketching things and paintings were neatly arrayed on the mantelpiece and chest of drawers.

After showing me her artistic work, she took me down the dark flight of stairs at the back of the house to the kitchen, where the Pluck family carried on most of their communal life. But I was soon ushered into the semi-basement parlour at the front of the house where a table was laid. Pluckie's mother had pre-pared exactly the kind of substantial meal that Mum provided when I got home from work each day – meat and vegetables followed by pudding, and tea to drink with it. We sat each side of a largish table and were waited on by Mrs Pluck, which gave a slightly formal tone to the occasion. Hard as I tried, nothing would induce Mrs Pluck to stay for more than a minute with us, let alone to sit down; nor would she hear of either of us lifting a finger to help. At the same time, her bustling about made it clear how much work was involved. Smiling and hospitable though she seemed, I knew that at some deeper level she resented the extra work inviting me home had caused her, just as I remembered my mother had done on a memorable oc-casion when I was still at school and had persuaded her to let me invite Ben to tea.

The faults and failings of our parents, especially our mothers, had been one of the things Pluckie and I most enjoyed confiding to each other. But I had come to realize that in spite of much common ground Pluckie's relationship with her mother was different from the one I had with mine. In my eyes, Mum had

many irritating habits, particularly that of putting Dad or the
'family's' interest before mine, but I had never doubted that, in
her way, she loved me. What is more, I had assumed that this
was something all mothers felt for their children, and something that all children had a right to expect. But Pluckie
believed that her mother did not, and never had, loved her. Her
only happy memories, she told me, of her earliest childhood
were of the time she spent with foster parents because, for some
reason I can no longer recall, her mother could not, or would
not, care for her. This was hard to believe, but there was no
difficulty in seeing that our mothers were certainly different in
appearance. Mum was tall, and in her young days had been
slim, although she now cheerfully – and I thought far too
complacently – accepted that the 'middle-aged spread' had set
in. But with her upright bearing, tobacco-coloured hair and
velvety brown eyes she was still, when dressed up, a Junoesque
figure. In comparison, Mrs Pluck was diminutive. Small boned
and bright-eyed, she was quick-moving and sharp in manner.
When she smiled, her small face was transformed into a girlish
prettiness, but she did not smile very often according to Pluckie.
Her life had been hard, and she had made it harder. She was
one of those women who seem to have a grim taste for gnawing
at their own wounds. One of the earliest of these for her had
been inflicted in childhood. She had been a bright girl from a
poor home who, against the odds of the time, won a scholarship
to a grammar school. She was not allowed to take it up, and this
lost opportunity was one of the deadliest drops in her fulsome
cup of bitterness. Later, when she married, the fates seemed
briefly to be smiling on her, for she had captivated a most
desirable man. As a skilled dental technician, Mr Pluck offered
the prospect of a married life of modest security and, for
Lambeth, relatively high status. Before long, these hopes too
were dashed when Mr Pluck began to spend as much time at
the pub as at home. The arrival of children – first Daphne, then
Pluckie, then much later Edward – inevitably meant more
worry and hardship. Already a martyr to her own high standards of housekeeping, and striving to maintain the family's
precarious hold on respectability, Mrs Pluck found mother-
hood more a burden than a blessing. All three of her children
were to prove both talented and clever. She took pride in their

achievements; but there was always her own bitterness to mar any joy. Having heard a good deal about this woman before I met her, I was intent on getting into her good books if I could, and I knew that the best hope of doing so was by lavish appreciation of her hospitality. I was gushing about the meal and her generosity in inviting me, with all the difficulties of rationing. At the same time, I appreciated that I could not possibly put her to this kind of trouble every week. I was pretty sure, that despite my polite talk (which made Mrs Pluck's face light up), if I did come every week – as Pluckie had suggested – it would certainly add to the endless complaints that Pluckie already had to put up with from her mother.

Half-way through our tea the parlour door burst open and Pluckie's elder sister came in. She had just arrived home and wanted to meet me, as I did her, each having heard about the other from Pluckie. Daphne was a primary-school teacher, a fair young woman positively sizzling with vitality. She had her mother's quick way of speaking but not her Cockney accent because, like Pluckie, Daphne had been to Greycoat Hospital, the prestigious girls' grammar school in Westminster. On this occasion her normal bubbling humour was mixed with agitation because she had mislaid the handkerchief in which she kept her engagement ring hidden. The engagement was a secret I knew about already. I also knew the reason it was secret. Her fiancé, Eric, was a local lad from a poor family in the neighbourhood. He lived with his parents in a street that was notoriously disreputable in that part of Lambeth. The family and the street were of just the kind from which Mrs Pluck had escaped and to which she fervently hoped never to return. When she heard through local tittle-tattle that her favourite daughter, of whose success in becoming a teacher she was so proud, had been seen about with Eric, she was more than angry. She was in a frenzy of rage. To her it must have seemed as if all her sacrifices were to prove in vain, all her hopes for Daphne under threat. To make things worse, Eric, as the whole neighbourhood knew, was an avowed conscientious objector. This was something that lined up Mr Pluck, for once, with his wife. The thought of having a conscientious objector for a son-in-law in patriotic, bomb-stricken Lambeth was too shameful to contemplate. Torn between love of her family and Eric (whose pacifist views she

shared), Daphne continued her romance in secret. Pluckie
could shed no light on the missing hanky, but managed to
reassure Daphne that it could not have been found by their
mother who, since our return, had been in an unusually
amenable humour. I heard some time later from Pluckie that
the ring turned up.

I did not see young Edward then because at that time he was
still an evacuee. He returned home some months afterwards. It
was Daphne who insisted with a determination quite as inflex-
ible as her mother's that the disruptions of war must not be
allowed to stop Edward getting a good education. Twelve years
older than her brother, Daphne became a kind of second
mother who supervised his homework and pushed him on and
widened his interests. Under Daphne's influence he soon became a favoured chorister at Southwark Cathedral, obtained a
place at a grammar school and started on the ladder to fame
and fortune. He was a lively boy who, as well as his musical
ability, seemed to have inherited his father's happy-go-lucky
temperament. This resemblance did not prevent (and indeed
perhaps partly explained) Mrs Pluck's more affectionate and
indulgent manner with Edward.

Vivid amongst Pluckie's earliest memories was that of full
sets of grinning, pink and white dentures lined up along the
kitchen mantelpiece, but by the time I got to know her, and for
reasons unknown to me, Mr Pluck was no longer the skilled
dental technician whom her mother had been so proud to catch
for a husband. Although he continued to help friends and
neighbours when their dentures were in need of repair or
replacements, Mr Pluck had given up this occupation to
become a bus-conductor.

With Mr Pluck's lucrative dental work in addition to his
regular earnings on the buses, the Pluck family could have had
a relatively comfortable standard of living but for the fact that
Mr Pluck spent so much of his leisure – and therefore his money
– in the pub. How much he had been driven there by his wife's
ways or the sheer incompatibility of their marriage, who can
say. What is certain is that Mr Pluck was by nature and
upbringing a most gregarious man. He had grown up in a pub,
and liked nothing better than playing the piano for the sing-
songs which at that time could cast such a rosy glow over the

harshness and pains of daily life. On the buses he could delight passengers with his Cockney repartee and unfailing good humour and helpfulness. It must have been far more attractive to a man of his temperament to be in the thick of life on the buses rather than working alone in a backroom workshop, and to enjoy the social life of the pub than to suffer the biting tongue of his wife at home. Small, with a red face and perky manner, Mr Pluck was a character such as Dickens might have created. It was a joy to find him at home; within minutes he would always have us convulsed in laughter. It was impossible to tire of his stories about the strange things that happened on buses. It was his way of telling them that made them so funny. One of my favourites was of the day when a woman passenger cried out that a thick, reddish-brown liquid was dripping down on her through the floor of the upper deck. Assuring the agitated woman that the liquid was paint, not blood, Mr Pluck pounded upstairs to find and then tackle the unfortunate and inoffensive-looking man responsible: ''Ere mate, what's this? I've got a passenger being dripped on below.' Mr Pluck's description of the complexities of placating the woman downstairs, whose alarm had by then changed to anger, and explanation of how successfully to remove a leaking tin of paint from the top deck of a bus, brought out the best of his comic and narrative skills. At such times even Mrs Pluck's icy hostility towards her husband would thaw into a bright smile that reflected not only amusement but something like pride.

6

Moving House

Our move from Lampmead Road to Taunton Road which, as I
said earlier, was just two streets away, opened up a new life for
Mum and Dad. For them the Blitz marked the start of the best
and happiest years of their marriage. The depressing inter-war
years of too little money, too little space and the recurrent
nightmare of unemployment were at last left behind – part of a
sad past on which they were only too pleased to turn their
backs. Generally too immersed in my own affairs to pay much
attention to Mum and Dad's, I could not help noticing that
they were getting on with each other a good deal better. Even
when Dad arrived home a bit boozy, it no longer provoked the
bad humours of old. I can see now that the first weeks after we
moved must for them have been a kind of long-delayed honeymoon, but on that Saturday when I burst into the living-room
and found them making love in Dad's fireside chair I was
deeply shocked. My face as I turned round to flounce out of the
room said more than any words could have done of my disgust.
Scrambling off Dad's lap and struggling to adjust her clothing,
Mum managed to express her own indignation before I had
time to get out of the room: 'You're not supposed to be here!
You said you wouldn't be back till five!' These were hardly
mollifying words in my ears. That a mother and father, at their
age – they were still in their forties! – should be interested in
each other sexually was bad enough. But to carry on like that,
downstairs and in broad daylight, was unspeakable. I was on
the brink of awakening to sexual passion, so to me it was a
new-minted pleasure that ought to belong exclusively to the
young.

The pleasures of sex were not the only thing that the move
had reinvigorated for my parents. Mum had always backed up

Dad in his work in any way she could, it was part and parcel of her deference to the primary importance of the male bread-winner, but now that the war had given Dad's building work a new importance she was to discover that it had extended her role in it too. Throughout the day there were callers at the door to be dealt with and, later on, telephone inquiries as well. Quick to adapt, and relishing her own as much as Dad's importance, Mum soon became expert at taking down messages, assessing priorities and in general acting as Dad's right hand. Her natural amiability and inveterate interest in other people's lives proved invaluable; and so too did her conviction that her husband must be protected from unreasonable demands from customers. To hear her talking it was as if Dad's services were a matter of grace and favour, for which Mum's goodwill in arranging an audience might be crucial. A caller had to be very important to be invited into the house, and most of Mum's interviews took place on the doorstep. Someone who was really well known, or who wished to discuss a very complicated matter, was occasionally invited in, but only into the hall, and more often than not this occurred only in cold weather when Mum's main interest was to shut the front door to 'keep out the cold'.

In fact, Dad did now have an 'office', the small box-room upstairs above the hall. It was just big enough to take an old desk and a cumbersome Victorian swivelling chair that Dad had 'found' somewhere. Later in the war, but after I had more or less left home, Dad even acquired a 'secretary' to help cope with the piles of paperwork that the war damage and bureaucracy jointly generated. The poor thing – a weedy, pasty-faced little fourteen-year-old girl – passed long, lonely hours in this 'office' cubby-hole, broken only when Mum took pity on her and called her downstairs for a cup of tea.

Mum continued to deal with most of the callers but had no taste for 'office work', which she regarded as far less important than her housekeeping tasks. Dad too spent little time in the 'office', preferring to do as much of his part of the paperwork as he could sitting in his armchair by the fire in the hour or two after his dinner before he went off on his evening visit to the pub.

When he was not out on a job, Dad was usually to be found in his yard, where there was always something to be done. The yard beyond our small back garden was a large, L-shaped space with several ramshackle sheds and a low brick building which Dad said had once been a pigsty. Dad had never been a gardener because at Lampmead Road that had been Grandad's undisputed domain. But he proved to have inherited his father's green fingers. Inspired, like thousands of others, by the slogan *Dig for Victory*, he decided to turn the space between the sheds and the pigsty into a kitchen garden where he could grow tomatoes, marrows, onions, peas, cucumbers, cabbages, beans and lettuces to enliven the rations. Even the old pigsty played its part: one year it provided so many mushrooms it was hard to dispose of them. Without refrigerators, let alone freezers, none of this abundant harvest could be stored for long. What we could not eat ourselves had to be passed on to friends, neighbours and anyone else Mum could find to take the excess.

With the derelict school on one side of the yard, the playground of our little local park on the other, and the bomb-site at the end, it was not long before Dad decided that he must get a dog to guard his property. Floss, our pedigree wire-haired terrier, had become far too much Mum's pampered pet to be used for this purpose, so Dad got a mongrel puppy from one of his widespread contacts. I named him 'Dizzy' because his drooping black ears and mournful brown eyes reminded me of a picture of Disraeli I had seen in one of my history books at school. To me Disraeli had seemed one of the more interesting though utterly remote figures from the past that we learnt about at my school. I should have been astonished had I realized that Grandad had been my age – nineteen – when Disraeli died and would surely have had opinions about him, had I only thought to ask.

Dad was always an early riser, and one of his earliest tasks was to go out through the back door, through the side gate in the fence that marked off the garden from the driveway, and walk up it to reach the yard. At the sight of Dad, Dizzy would emerge from his kennel against the school wall, run as far as his chain would allow towards Dad, and whine furiously. He had to be kept on a running chain because, although always affectionate to those he knew, he was prone to bite those he didn't. However long the run, a chained dog is a frustrated one, and Dizzy was no exception. Unless Dad was with him in the yard, he spent a lot of his time running frenziedly back and forth, making his protest by barking. Almost anything would set him off – a noise in the park or the ruined school, the arrival of a caller or the teasing visit from a local cat. It was an irritation in the daytime, but even worse at night. My room was at the back of the house, overlooking the garden and the yard beyond. I could almost always sleep through air raids, but not through these barking fits or, even worse, when Dizzy howled. Mum was as irritated as I was at having her sleep disturbed in this way (she and Dad had the other back bedroom), but Dad invariably slept through it. Sometimes Mum would get angry enough to try to wake him. 'There must be someone up the yard. Listen to that dog!' I would hear her say in loud exasperation. But this did no good. Dad would grunt and then begin to snore again. Mum's only recourse was to get out of her warm bed, open the window and shriek into the darkness, 'Go in your kennel, Dizzy' – or sometimes just 'Shut up!' Neither usually had much effect. It was amazing that the neighbours put up with it. They hardly ever complained. Maybe they all slept as soundly as Dad did.

When I had nothing better to do, I liked to walk up the yard to let Dizzy off the chain and have a game with him. And whenever Dad was there, I never minded going to call him for his dinner and finding out what he was doing. Tall and stringy, often still wearing his trilby hat and 'working' suit, he was always busy at something – stacking wood or bricks, shovelling a great pile of sand, hammering or sawing, mixing paint, sorting out his tools – but never too busy to give a nod of his head in my direction, with that wry half-smile which lit up his blue eyes and momentarily softened his bony, weathered face. He was never around at lunch-time. For him, lunch was a pint of beer either at his local or a pub near to where his work had taken him that day. This suited Mum, who considered making two meals a day for the family quite enough to get on with.

It was only at weekends that we all sat down together for our meals. On weekday mornings we had breakfast according to Mum's carefully managed routine. She called us so that we arrived in turn downstairs at about ten-minute intervals. This was supposed to give each of us time to wash at the kitchen sink without tripping over each other. In spite of Mum's careful timing, there were days when I did find myself too close on Wal's heels, which always meant a bad-tempered start to the day. I would complain to Wal of his tardiness and he would provokingly refuse to hurry. We never used the 'bathroom' because Dad's version of this in the attic did not include a hand-basin or a supply of hot water except from the geyser over the bath. Nor did we have running hot water downstairs either. Dad washed in cold water, night and morning, but Mum always had hot water boiled up in the kettle for the rest of us to tip into the bowl in the deep porcelain sink.

It was my job before going up to bed at night to 'put on the cloth' and get out the sugar-bowl, marmalade and a few bits of cutlery from the sideboard ready for breakfast. This took barely a minute, but was somehow important in Mum's timetable and, if I forgot, it led to angry recriminations in the morning which I preferred to avoid. By the time I sat down to the table, Dad and Joe had gone off to work and Wal was almost ready to follow.

In the evenings the routine was much the same. Mum liked to be given a time at which she could expect each of us home so that she could have our dinners ready to serve up immediately we each got in. I would usually be eating my pudding by the time Wal sat down, with Joe following soon after. Dad's return was less predictable and, although Mum invariably asked him 'What time will you be back?', more often than not she had to be satisfied with a mumbled 'Shan't be late' or 'About usual'.

In spite of the rationing and the scarcity of good things off rations, Mum contrived somehow to provide and cook for us much as she had always done. It was a matter of making the best of things – at which she had had plenty of practice before the war began, she said. By picking up tips from Ministry of Food leaflets, as well as her friends, she soon knew how to make dried eggs palatable and – in *her* crisp and golden batter – even Spam fritters became quite a treat. By keeping in with shop-keepers she also managed to find enough sugar and fruits and fats to make the boiled or baked puddings which, like her mother before her, she often served up to round off our dinners. Looking after her family in the way she thought proper was certainly made harder for Mum because of the war. Sometimes, she complained, she spent the whole morning shopping and queuing. It demanded both patience (which was not one of her qualities) and an overriding sense of her priorities (in which the family came first, of course). She was always ready to dash from one place to another whenever the news got round that this or that scarce commodity had 'just come in'.

Mum's idea of managing her family owed much to her own mother's influence. She had grown up in a small village where life was not easy, but cosy and cluttered; and so primitive in amenities that even water, which had to be pumped up from a well, was not to be used too freely. This must have left her with the conviction that spit could be used as a convenient alternative. When my brothers and I were very young she had always been quick to clean up our dirty faces by spitting on her hanky, or even on the hem of her skirt or pinafore. And whenever she had to wash or tidy up in a hurry it was always 'It'll have to make do with a spit and a promise'.

The war and the rationing proved to be the stimulus for Mum's invention of a new way of making use of spit. Bread in our house was always buttered on the loaf before a slice was cut. To my horror, one day, complaining about the butter ration and at the same time of the difficulty of spreading it thinly enough when it was cold and hard, Mum popped a lump into her mouth, chewed it a bit and then spat it on to the bread. She had found a way of making the ration go further!

As a child I had always hated Mum's makeshift 'spit wash', although mainly because of her roughness rather than for reasons of hygiene or fastidiousness. This new habit with the butter seemed far worse, but I knew it would be unwise to make any protest. Unfortunately, although I did not dare say anything, Mum saw enough in what she called 'that toffee-nosed look' on my face to make her angry. To her, my distaste was a rejection of the natural and proper closeness of the relationship that ought to exist between us. It was the sort of thing that would provoke her to say, 'If you don't like it here, you can get out!' At such times, this was exactly what I felt I should like to do, but the trouble was I had no confidence that I could. For one thing, I believed – perhaps because Mum had told me so more than once – that I could not afford to live anywhere but at home. I also knew, in spite of Mum's harsh words, that any serious attempt of mine to move out, unless it was to get married, would shock and distress both her and Dad. And even if I could have plucked up the courage to hurt them like this, how to go about finding somewhere else was beyond me.

It was just as well, therefore, that most of the time Mum and I got on much better than we had during the difficult years when I was at the grammar school and in the throes of early adolescence. And with Dad my relationship was warmer than it had ever been. Neither his mocking, deflating comments on my looks or my clothes or my views could conceal his pride and pleasure in his only daughter.

It was not long after I went to the bank that Dad had brought home an old typewriter he had picked up somewhere. It was a heavy old machine, probably Victorian, which I could barely lift. But once he realized that I had I learned to type a bit, Dad saw that this could lighten the burden of the job estimates he had to prepare, and which until then he had written out by hand. It also meant that Dad could benefit from my superior knowledge of spelling. I was not very fast, and the results of my efforts were not by any means professional-looking, but they were quite good enough in Dad's eyes. And for me it was at least much easier than an earlier experience I had had when Kit had asked me to type out an article for him entitled 'Britain's Supremacy in the Banking World'. I had felt honoured by this task, but it proved an onerous one; the more so as I could make little sense of the contents.

Almost as difficult was the task that fell on me of composing a letter about Joe's work problem. When he had returned home from evacuation, Joe started work as an apprentice at a local firm of electrical engineers. He soon realized that the apprenticeship was not what he had been led to believe. It proved to mean not only long hours, low pay and hard work but offered him little prospect of attaining skills. He began to look for something else, but when he found another possible job, as a trainee post-office engineer, it transpired that under war regulations he could not change his job unless he could get an official 'green card'. This was refused on the grounds that he was already in work of national importance. Because of his attempt to get the vital green card, Joe became the victim of the foreman's ill will and so increasingly unhappy. He was only a teenage boy, and as he would be going from one sort of essential work to another, his – and our – sense of injustice grew strong. Talking about it at the pub drew forth the suggestion from one of Dad's cronies that the best thing for Joe to do was for him to leave his job, get a new one, and then ask for the card. So Joe stayed at home.

A few weeks later I arrived home from work to find the household in turmoil. A letter had come for Dad saying that if Joe did not return to work immediately, prosecution would follow and Dad would be liable to three months in prison. Mum was in tears. She was indignant at Joe's plight, but even more concerned at the threat to Dad. 'How could we manage if he went to prison?' she kept demanding. In the family conclave that followed, Wal suggested that Joe ought to go back to work 'but be so bloody awkward that they'll want you to go', whereas Dad and I were at one that we should dig our heels in and defy authority. What we all agreed was that exceptional action was called for: an appeal had to be made to higher authority. The task of composing the letter fell on me and, after hard work on the typewriter, interspersed with much family discussion across the dining-room table, a long and emotional appeal was sent off to Mr Ernest Bevin, Minister of Labour. It was the first time in my life that I had made a direct approach to the powers that be, and I felt greatly pleased with my effort.

A reply came not from the Minister but the local MP to whom the letter had been passed on. It was a disappointing response because although it expressed sympathy, it promised nothing. All ended well, however, when Joe, resigned by then to his fate, as he thought, made his way to the GPO to tell them he could not take up the interview he had been offered as he had been unable to get a green card. No doubt desperate for new recruits to take the place of the skilled engineers it had had to surrender to the Army, the GPO stepped in. The vital green card turned up. It proved in a sense to be Joe's passport to a far more varied and successful career than we could have dreamt of at that time.

By an odd quirk of fate, soon after the war Joe came briefly face to face with Ernest Bevin at the Foreign Office. Only recently demobbed from the Army, and by then an experienced signals engineer, Joe found himself ordered in bullying tones to 'hurry up and get out of my office'. Not surprisingly, it was an experience that did nothing to diminish Joe's prejudice against the great man.

Always out and about in the locality, Dad was a frequent caller at our former home after we moved. And in spite of the strains and resentments that had built up during the years when the family shared a house, Mum was still the daughter-in-law whom Gran and Grandad saw most. On weekdays she popped in often to give what help she could in shopping, and to ease the problems of rationing. Pete and Ken also often called round to see us; but although we were so near to them, Gran and Grandad never did. It was not so much resentment at our moving away, though I don't doubt that this rankled with Gran, but that it was not in their scheme of things. They saw their home as the centre of the family they had created and I don't think they ever visited any of their married sons, although all but one of the five surviving ones lived close by. On Sunday mornings Gran's kitchen continued to be the gathering-place for her sons and grandchildren – until, that is, the effects of the war gradually depleted the family circle.

7

In Pursuit of Culture

On the day I first went home with Pluckie we had spent so
much time talking that we were late setting off for Morley
College. Fortunately we hadn't far to go, and by running half
the way we arrived on time, but a little breathless. The session
was due to begin at six o'clock.

One of the things that had attracted me to come to this class
on philosophy with Pluckie was that the lecturer was to be the
renowned Professor C. E. M. Joad. An early version of a media
star, Joad was someone even Mum and Dad had heard of. He
was a regular member of *The Brains Trust*, then a popular
programme on the wireless, and articles by or about him
frequently appeared in the newspapers. I could hardly believe
that such a person would appear in the flesh before us this
evening, and the prospect was exciting.

I was impressed at once with Morley College. It was not
exactly grand, but the surroundings were harmonious and the
atmosphere somehow both serious and lively. Best of all, it did
not seem at all like school. Even the class-room, where there
was a blackboard, felt different as we sat down and waited. We
were by no means the first to arrive, but found two chairs side
by side and looked surreptitiously round at our fellow students.
There was only one other girl, making three with Pluckie and
myself, but the class was obviously popular, for there were
plenty of men, one of whom was Pluckie's beau, James
Elgin.

When Joad arrived some twenty minutes late, he was not a
bit as I had imagined him. Misled by the pernickety tone of his
voice that I knew from listening to *The Brains Trust*, I had
thought he would be a dapper, mousy-haired and rather elderly
man, but he looked buoyantly middle aged. His short hair stuck

out like horns, one each side of the middle parting. It was white, like his well-trimmed beard. This, far from making him look old, was in attractive contrast to his lightly tanned, unlined face and small, bright eyes. His voice too was pleasanter than I had expected, and what on the wireless had come over to me as pernickety now emerged as a slight lisp. As he spoke, his eyes darted round the room, glinting with an amusement that suggested he did not take himself – or perhaps us – very seriously; and from time to time his tongue darted forward like a lizard's. Having arrived so late, Joad gave us no more than a quick review of the syllabus for the term before announcing that his first lecture would be in a fortnight's time. As he rushed out of the class-room, indignant mutterings from the braver spirits followed him. Everyone felt cheated.

Deprived of our intellectual feast, Pluckie and I were delighted when James Elgin proposed that we should join him for a cup of coffee. We caught a bus to Trafalgar Square and went into Lyons Corner House which as always was buzzing with people and, despite the black-out outside, glowing with light. We found a table, ordered our coffee from the nippy (waitress) when she came over, and settled down to a discussion. James took over where Joad had left off by telling us more about what he thought the course might cover. It wasn't long before we were recklessly splashing in deep philosophical waters. We argued furiously over the – to me – novel concept of 'the absolute'. When James mildly pointed out that 'Probably there is no such thing', Pluckie protested indignantly that this in itself was an absolute. Completely out of my depth, I floundered first this way and then that before Pluckie joined me in conceding humbly to James Elgin's superior logic.

Not surprisingly, I found myself equally out of my depth at Joad's philosophy lectures and decided to abandon the class. Pluckie continued, but suggested that I should try another course, which she had also begun, on psychology. More interested in an evening in her company than anything else, I agreed to try it. She told me that the lecturer for this class was a woman who had 'written books'. I had never heard of Mrs Amber Blanco White but, as she was an author, I went along to the new class with the same high hopes of coming face to face with eminence as I had with Professor Joad.

Tall and skinny, with gappy, slightly protruding teeth, Mrs Blanco White was plain and middle aged, but charmed us with her humour and vivacity. At one session, which was on the importance of the sexual side of life to mental health, she ended up miming in front of the class various positions which she said could be used to make sexual intercourse more fun. Whether male or female, it is probable that at that time most of the students were, like Pluckie and me, still virgins who for the first time were publicly and unembarrassedly enjoying a discussion on sex.

In those idle moments of chat that take place in a class before the lecturer arrives, the rumour had gone round that this plain married woman believed in 'free love' and had had many affairs. It was only after her wicked demonstration that I came to see that this could indeed have been true.

Amber Blanco White set out to broaden the narrow horizons of students like me, and she made us work as well as laugh, marking the essays she set us with stimulating comments. She was a proponent of free love who advised us never to tell a spouse about a lover, and pointed out that living together as lovers did not have to mean being married. None were more fervent in demands for equality of the sexes than Pluckie and I, but we were as much concerned about inequalities in the home – and the office – as in bed. We believed that women ought to be allowed the same sexual freedom as men outside marriage, but although we claimed not to be much in favour of marriage, we believed in faithfulness within it. What is more, in spite of our wish to be modern and free, this had not weakened our vaguer romantic hopes of finding the kind of perfect love that seemed to be the stuff of much of the poetry and literature which nourished us. Amongst such literature was the work of Vera Brittain, to which Pluckie introduced me. *Testament of Youth*, with its moving account of a girl's struggle against dull parents to get educated, was something with which we could fervently identify. So too was the story of her passionate and ill-fated romance with a young officer who was soon killed in the Great War. Romantics that we were, we could not fail to see ourselves as being caught up in a potentially similar cataclysmic course, and Pluckie was able to identify as well with Vera Brittain's pacifism. We looked on revered women like Vera Brittain and her friend Winifred Holtby as models in whose footsteps we might follow.

It was probably at Morley College that we found out about a rally to be held one Saturday afternoon in Trafalgar Square, recognizing that this was just the kind of thing we should be supporting. The rally was organized by some group, unknown to me, which was demanding equal compensation for women who suffered war injuries. We arrived early – the meeting was to start at two o'clock – and although we were by no means the first, we managed to wriggle our way to the very front of the crowd. At the bottom of Nelson's Column, between two of the Landseer lions, microphones and chairs were already set up awaiting the arrival of the platform party. Just behind, three women were discussing the question on which the speakers were soon to address us. The name 'Eileen' came up frequently in their talk. It became clear as we listened that Eileen was a relative of one of the women, and that they had come along to make their protest on her behalf. She had lost a leg in the Blitz, and they were angry that because she was a woman she was getting less compensation than a man would.

The sun shone brightly, the crowd grew larger and the platform began to fill. It was to be an all-party meeting and we recognized well-known politicians such as Nancy Astor and Edith Summerskill. There were others, too, like Harriet Cohen, the pianist, who had also agreed to speak. A young woman wearing dark glasses was helped on to the platform by a man – the only male up there. They sat close together, and the girl had her face half turned away from the crowd. It was when Edith Summerskill was coming to the end of a typically forceful speech that she called upon the girl to stand and remove her dark glasses. Looking up at her from our position just beneath the platform, we were appalled to see that her closed eyelids were stretched like thin parchment over empty sockets. Her chin was also pockmarked with scars and there was a deeper scar across her cheek which pulled up her mouth to one side. She was our age – nineteen. Nothing could make up for what this girl had lost, but she seemed to have none of the bitterness I imagined I should have felt. It was but small consolation that,

with continued pressure of the kind the meeting was demon-
strating, she – and others like her – would eventually receive
compensation equal to that of similarly injured men.

Not all our activities were so serious. Although Pluckie was
not interested, as I still was, in trivial pursuits such as going to
local dances, the cinema or pub, we shared a taste for exhibitions and concerts; and for both of us going to a meeting at
Conway Hall was thrilling, whether it was to hear Mary
Sutherland speaking on 'Women at War' or Victor Gollancz on
'Victory in Europe'. There was always something to learn or
find out on such occasions, and to discuss earnestly between
ourselves afterwards. Could Mary Sutherland *really* be right in
thinking that, although women had flocked into the factories to
help the war effort, they would still prefer to be just housewives
at home? Could there possibly be a danger, as Gollancz feared,
that we would ruin the future prospects for Europe by again
imposing harshly retributive terms on the Germans when at
last we defeated them?

Britain at the time was a long way from peace of any kind,
and this uncertainty about the future made us more determined
to squeeze what we could out of our wartime lives. Believing
that the world of banking was boring and not one we would
have chosen to be in if we had had a wider choice, it unfortunately seemed likely that we could be trapped in it indefinitely.
As a reserved occupation banking was subject to controls,
which meant one could not leave without official permission.
This did not stop me from having recurrent longings to get out
of the bank into a more interesting job, and whenever I could I
borrowed Mr Dallinger's *Daily Telegraph* to look through the
situations vacant columns. I was attracted one day by a most
unusual advert: 'Girl 16–20 years wanted for head studies.' It
had been a difficult day on a new ledger to which I had been
temporarily transferred, and I had also had the bad news – for
me – from my old friend Averil that she was getting married and
going to set up home near her husband's Army base. On
impulse, I rushed out during my tea-break and rang the
number given in the advertisement. A well-spoken male voice
at the other end of the line asked me my age and for details of my
colouring and height and, apparently finding these satisfactory,
invited me to call at his 'studio' for interview. I told him where I

worked and that I would come along after I had finished at the bank.

Later I found a chance to confide in Pluckie. I thought she would be excited at the prospect of my going to see an 'artist' whose improbable name was Captain Palmerston. But her blue eyes opened wide with what looked more like alarm mixed with a disconcerting hint of disbelief. 'I could just not turn up,' I said, but such irresponsible behaviour was not the kind to commend itself to Pluckie. The compromise we decided on was that she should come along with me to give me courage, and wait outside to make sure that I emerged safely from this daring adventure.

We were lucky with buses and arrived at our destination in West Kensington at what turned out to be a tall Edwardian house of red brick. Outside the front door I waved and grinned at Pluckie as she walked away to wait on a nearby corner. Seeing that she had taken up her position, I turned round and knocked on the door with a display of bravado. If there had been much of a delay I should have soon fled, but only seconds elapsed before the door was opened and I was face to face with Captain Palmerston. He was a plumpish, middle-aged man of a muddy complexion. He was wearing a blue check shirt with a bow-tie and his navy blue trousers were held up by a necktie round his waist. In my eyes this was a sufficiently unconventional garb to confirm the man's artistic credentials.

I have no idea how Captain Palmerston had been so prompt to open the door, for he made clear that his studio was on the third floor! As we climbed the stairs I could see that the house was either empty or almost wholly unfurnished, which seemed a bit eerie. It was therefore a relief to me to find that the studio, when we reached it, was exactly as I imagined a studio should be. It had a very high ceiling and three huge windows along one wall. Paintings and photographs were propped against or pinned on other walls. Covering part of the large area of stained floor-boards was a worn black carpet, and in front of an empty fireplace a shabby armchair. In the very centre of the room stood a big easel, and not far away from it dangled a human skeleton.

As he had done all the way up the stairs, Captain Palmerston talked a lot. My job at the bank launched him into a minor discourse on the cruelty of 'shutting up young people in offices' – something he could not have *endured* himself, for he had always been 'wild' and at twenty was 'going mad in South America'. He told me about his previous models. There was Magda, who had been with him twelve years and did not want to leave to get married at all until he insisted that 'she had better go while she had the chance'. Then there was 'darling little Phoebe', who had, poor dear, been killed in an air raid. I heard about his country house which the Army had 'taken over for a miserable rent and would no doubt rip to pieces'; and the story of the skeleton, which the Captain used to keep in his bedroom 'because it was so lovely waking up to see her grinning at me in the mornings'.

The purpose of my visit inspired further commentary. I had 'a good head' and a lovely long neck and long hands. But I was, he thought, much too thin – probably anaemic and not very robust, he said, asking as an aside whether I would consider figure as well as head modelling (a suggestion I cautiously declined). The more he talked the odder it became, until I began to feel quite dazed. By the end of yet another story about a girl who had cut her throat in the studio – 'the stain is still under the carpet' – I was no longer clear whether the Captain was talking about the 'sticky end' he had earlier told me had been the fate of the skeleton or another girl who had passed through his life or his studio! What I *was* sure of was that it was high time for me to leave (as, with hindsight, I can see Captain Palmerston had probably decided very much earlier).

Once outside, I raced along to the corner where for almost an hour Pluckie had been patiently, but increasingly anxiously, waiting. When I reached her my legs felt weak, not from the sprint along the road but from a mixture of fear and incredulity I had managed to suppress. These sensations were soon replaced by mirth as I recounted in what became increasingly hilarious detail my bizarre story. Sometimes it was hard to convince Pluckie that I was not just making it all up to amuse her; and it was rather a let-down to have to admit that I had not been offered the job. All I could say was that when I left the house Captain Palmerston had told me he would write and let me know about the head modelling. But, needless to say, no word came.

Of course I told Andrew about my visit to the studio, which inspired him to further artistic efforts of his own. He decided to paint a portrait of me wearing my warden's steel helmet and to enter it in one of the wartime exhibitions. The art treasures of the national collections had been put away for the duration, and perhaps this partly explained the explosion of amateur talent at the time. The war seemed to unleash all kinds of creativity in all sorts of people, who were often inspired by the dramatic scenes brought to everyday life.

One of the exhibitions where Andrew's work was on show was at the National Gallery, where two thousand drawings and paintings from members of the forces (of which the Home Guard was by then considered a part) were on display. The fact that the dreary little catalogue printed on yellowish wartime paper said that there had been 'no selection on merit, everything which space will accommodate has been displayed' could not diminish my pride and pleasure at seeing my portrait hanging on a wall of the illustrious building. Neither Andrew nor I could persuade Mum and Dad that it was worth the effort to travel from Lee to see it; but during its brief hour of glory, Pluckie and I more than once went along to stand in front of it (I was half afraid and half hoping that I might be recognized). On another occasion I took Averil along. She said she did not think it was much like me. This was disconcerting because, in spite of my wish to be flattered, it was just what I thought myself.

8

Breaking Down Conventions

When I first started at the bank it was the unquestioned custom for all female staff to wear stockings. Most of us still wore hats, but these could be a matter of personal choice, whereas stockings could not. Even in summer and the hottest of heat waves no one, especially under Auntie's vigilant eye, would have risked defying the unwritten rule on stockings. With clothes rationing stockings became a problem because of the heavy demand they made on limited clothing coupons. It was a problem that more and more women who were not bank employees were solving by going bare-legged in good weather, but Auntie was adamant that this practice would not do for the banking profession. She pointed out that we did not have to wear *silk* stockings (which were in any case getting harder and harder to find); we could do as she did and buy longer-lasting lisle ones. Finding acceptably fine lisle stockings was almost as difficult, but at first no one dared to defy Auntie's edict. Then someone discovered that a stocking make-up had come out which, it was said, could be indistinguishable from the real thing if carefully applied. From then on a favourite topic of conversation over tea or coffee was whether this could be the answer. One difficulty foreseen was that, as all decent stockings had clocks above the heel, as well as a seam running all the way up the back of the leg, it would be very difficult to get away with it under the eagle eye of Auntie. But increasingly concerned about my dwindling store of clothing coupons, I decided that the time had come to have a go.

With jovial encouragement from Mum and Dad, who were amused by the whole daft procedure, I set to work on my legs one evening after supper. It proved to be a laborious task. I began by smoothing the brownish cream all over my legs to a safe distance above my knees. The leg cream was claimed to be waterproof, so I had no fears that it would come off in the night (although Mum was, with some reason, less sanguine than I was about the prospect of its 'ending up all over the sheets'). What was more difficult was putting on the clocks and the seams, which had to be improvised with an eyebrow pencil, and carefully retouched in the morning where they had smudged.

Reassured by the family that the illusion was completely convincing, I went off to work happily confident that it really did look as if I had stockings on. I was indeed so proud of the result that I could not resist telling one or two of my fellow clerks. The rumour that Miss Noble was *not* wearing stockings spread fast round the building. Before the morning was over not only were my legs the focus of all eyes, but the excuse for some of the more daring male staff to try to take a closer look. Returning from my coffee-break I heard scuffling behind me, and on turning round saw several not-so-young men half crawling along the corridor behind me! It was a Saturday morning, a time when there was always a more light-hearted atmosphere at the bank, and apart from the fear of an irate approach from Auntie, I enjoyed the joke as much as anyone. Today this would surely be called 'sexual harassment'.

I can't in fact claim that I was the first to break the bank's stocking rule. It is very likely that some other girl had done the same thing before me, but with more discretion. In any case, the custom had been breeched, so that soon after, so long as leggy nudity was discreetly toned down with make-up, bare legs became acceptable. Stockings, however, remained a problem.

This was something of which Don was well aware when he reappeared at the bank one morning. It was quite some time since I had seen him. After being 'called up' he had been selected for training as a pilot and sent off for six months to Canada to complete his training. 'Don Faversham's looking for you. Have you seen him?' asked Amy one day as our paths crossed in the main corridor, she on her way to her coffee-break and I returning from mine. A few minutes later Don appeared beside me, smiling quizzically down and seeming taller and even fairer than he had before enlisting. He looked splendidly debonair in his pilot officer's uniform, on which the prized badge of wings gleamed white. We chatted a little, while Auntie looked on benignly, recognizing that our boys on leave must be allowed special privileges. Don had three weeks' leave before being posted to Bomber Command, he said, and wanted to know when I was free. I had to tell him that I was leaving after work that day for a week's holiday in North Wales. 'Well,' said Don, with an impressive confidence which I felt must be the result of his enviable new experiences, 'I shall have to come too'. He added nonchalantly that he had brought back with him from Canada *eighteen* pairs of silk stockings. I was dismayed because I was forced to explain that I was going to Wales with Andrew. What with the glamour of Don's uniform and the temptation of the stockings, I set off to meet Andrew at the station with dampened enthusiasm. It was a bad start to what I had been looking forward to until then as another great new adventure.

Andrew's grandparents, with whom we went to stay, lived in a low, white-walled cottage on the edge of the town of Penmaenmawr. The cottage was very small, with only two bedrooms, so that Andrew had to sleep on the sofa in the cosy little living-room. From the front we could look down to the sea, and from behind we could look up to the mountains. No matter if it were wet or fine, we spent most of the week walking and climbing in the surrounding hills and mountains, taking a packed lunch with us and returning to the cottage for an evening meal. On our last day we set off to conquer Snowdon, undeterred by Grandfather's oft-repeated joke: 'What is the difference between the man who has been to Snowdon and the man who has not? One has seen the mist and the other has missed the scene.' We were lucky, because for us the sun was shining. By the time we reached the summit we were able to look down on golden streamers of cloud hanging like garlands around the mountain-side below us. I was intoxicated by the beauty of the Welsh scenery – the lakes, the mountain pools that fell down rock-faces like skeins of silver hair, the blue views across the Menai Straits to Anglesey and Puffin Island, the green fields and valleys, and even the mists and drenching rains. By the end of the week in such surroundings I was almost certain that Andrew was to be my one true love.

This did not stop me from neglecting him completely when

we returned to London. I had promised Don I would telephone him as soon as I got back, which I did. For a whole fortnight I spent most of my free time with him, listening enthralled to his account of life in the Canadian prairies, and delighting again in a round of visits to theatres and smart restaurants. While I had been in Wales, he told me, he had been seeing his first love, Sylvia. I had no objections – how could I? But I suffered a little at hearing that, as a result, half of the stockings had been given to her!

Don was insistent that we spent as much time together as we could. He was already facing the fact that in Bomber Command life expectation was short. He might not have much of a future or, indeed, any future at all. His parents probably feared this too, and were easily persuaded to let him borrow their Rover to drive me out to Box Hill. It was a glorious autumn day, and we wandered about happily on the green turf of the hill, along footpaths hedged with rusting foliage and red berries and ended up lunching at a picturesque restaurant by a water-mill.

In London again, Don accompanied Pluckie and me to a political meeting at the Garrick Theatre, where Michael Foot, Frank Owen and Harry Pollit were passionately arguing about the need for an offensive on the Western Front to help Russia. And for both of the weeks he was around, Doug came along with us to Amber Blanco White's psychology class at Morley College, where anyone in uniform was welcome to drop in when they could. By the time Don's leave ended I was nearly persuaded that I was at least as much in love with him as I was with Andrew. Don seemed to feel much the same about Sylvia and me – which meant, as I had hoped, that Don gave me the remaining stockings.

At the end of 1941 Japan attacked Pearl Harbor and brought America into the war. One lunchtime, not long after, I watched with other City workers the arrival of the first American troops as they marched along Princes Street on a ceremonial visit to the Mansion House. I was impressed by the height of the GIs, their healthy good looks and white teeth, as well as by their uniforms, which looked of finer material than the rough khaki worn by our 'other ranks'. What the future held seemed uncertain, but the dramatic events served to increase my discontent with the dull part I was playing in them. In spite of my having gone through the Blitz, the war to me was being fought anywhere but in London, and certainly not in a bank in the City. After work one gloomy day I walked all the way along Cheapside, Fleet Street and the Strand struggling to pluck up courage to join the WRNS, whose silky black stockings made their uniform particularly attractive to me. It was pouring with rain and, unable to find the recruiting office, I had to give up. I arrived home very wet and disconsolate.

A week or two later, retracing my steps, I did succeed in finding a recruitment office, but it was for the WAAF not the WRNS. I decided to give up hankering after the black stockings. I filled in the appropriate forms, with the help of a charming young corporal (who looked reassuringly attractive in her air-force blue uniform, notwithstanding thick, grey lisle stockings). By the time I got home I was already uneasy and dared not tell Mum and Dad. When a letter came from the Ministry of Employment to say that I was already doing 'work of national importance' and could not therefore be released for the services, I was happy I could forget about it.

Some weeks later, quite happily at work on my ledger, I looked up one day to find Auntie beside me. She said, 'Just run upstairs, dear' (the dangers and unpredictable disturbances caused by the Blitz had by this time driven us out of the banking hall to work below ground in the safes). 'Mr Iliffe wants to see you.' Thinking on the way that there must be some problem about the holiday rota he wanted to sort out, I knocked and went into 'the Box' very cheerfully.

His opening remark took me aback. 'Miss Noble, have you ever considered joining the services?'

It did not take much acumen on my part to realize that news had got back to the bank of my attempt to join up. I knew that here was a classic case where honesty was not just the best but the only possible policy. 'Yes,' I said quickly, 'but the Ministry tell me that I am already doing work of national importance.'

Volunteering for the services by young men could be seen as understandable, but I suspected that what I had done would be regarded as a slight mark against me – some kind of failure to put the bank's interests first. However, at my reply Mr Iliffe nodded and looked satisfied.

There was a pause, during which Mr Iliffe gazed at me standing on the other side of his large desk, while I noticed how the electric light gave a shiny, doll-like look to his smooth, pink complexion. The expression on his face combined good humour and shrewdness, but the half-lowered lids of his eyes warned me to be wary. 'Are you happy here?' he asked.

'Yes,' I answered, compromising a bit with the truth, 'but the work is boring.'

Mr Iliffe said amiably, 'All jobs are boring – even mine.'

I remarked drily that in that case I shouldn't mind changing places with him, at which Mr Iliffe continued to look amiable but pointed out that I was much too young to expect to be in his place. Inspired as much by his apparent good humour as by a rousing sense of injustice, I launched into an indignant monologue on the lack of prospects for women of any age at the bank. It was true, I rushed on to say, that because some of the men had gone into the forces women were now being given their work to do, but what would happen when the war was over and the men came back?

Mr Iliffe still managed to hold on to his smile, but by now he had turned his head slightly to one side. I had the feeling that for him this lively discussion had gone far enough, and I waited to be dismissed. But he had not finished yet. 'You are friendly with Mr Elgin, aren't you?' he said.

I don't know if my mouth dropped open, but I was certainly, if momentarily, dumbstruck. So much so that it was Mr Iliffe who felt obliged to break the silence, first by muttering something about not wanting to be personal, and then going on: 'Or should I say that you and Mr Elgin have similar views about things?'

Pulling myself together, I said quickly, 'No, we certainly haven't – he is a pacifist, for one thing, and I'm not.'

'Oh, you're not? Then what are you? A communist – you and little Miss Pluck?'

By now quite stunned at the turn the interview had taken, I denied this new charge.

Mr Iliffe's manner slipped again into a kind of avuncular good humour. 'I'm glad to hear that – little Miss Pluck is too pretty to be a communist – but what *are* you then? Pink Labour maybe?'

It was my turn to tease. 'We are surely *much* too young to have any opinions, Mr Iliffe,' I answered.

There was no longer a lot of warmth in the smile on Mr Iliffe's face as he picked up the appropriately pink-coloured note from staff department lying on his desk, but he slowly and deliberately tore it up. As he did so he said, 'I'm very glad we are not going to lose you, Miss Noble – and now I must not keep you from your work.'

I went out breezily, but I felt a bit like a fly that had narrowly escaped a spider's web.

Back in the safe, I was agog to tell Pluckie about what had happened. We agreed to walk over London Bridge together after work so that we could mull over it at leisure. I was rather pleased with my performance, and inclined to take it all as a joke now that it was behind me. Pluckie took it far more seriously, insisting she was not all surprised. James Elgin had frequently warned her, she said, that there was little the bank management did not know about its employees. What is more, James believed that because of his politics, and even more because of his pacifism, he was certainly under surveillance and probably suspected of being a spy. This all seemed far-fetched to me, although I could see that the bank might feel obliged to take *some* interest in James because promotion had to be based on knowledge about his reliability, and similar things. Yet for mere females like Pluckie and me, for whom careers with promotional prospects were not to be expected, what did it matter to management what we did outside office hours?

Then why, demanded Pluckie, had Iliffe cross-examined me as he did?

I said flippantly, 'It probably had more to do with Iliffe's nosiness than anything else.'

But I knew that, because of James, Pluckie was convinced there might indeed be some more sinister, perhaps officially inspired, motive behind it.

9

Love in Bloom

Dad's youngest brothers – the twins, Bern and Harold – were only about fourteen years old when I was born and, until they married, lived downstairs with Gran and Grandad and my two orphan cousins, Pete and Ken. Sharing the same house with us, as they then did, the twins were more like elder brothers than uncles to us and even as children we always called them simply by their Christian names.

Bern was the first to get married, and the wedding was a grand affair at which I was one of the four bridesmaids. But when Harold married his girl, Betty, she was already several months' pregnant and the couple just slipped off to the registry office and came back to our house afterwards. It was a fine summer's day and we all went into the garden so that someone could take a snap or two of the newly weds standing in front of one of Grandad's lilac bushes. The bride wore a navy crêpe dress with small white polka dots. The skirt of her dress, new for the wedding, was fashionably cut on the cross and clung pretty closely. This called forth some ribald joking from Dad and Grandad about Betty's rounded belly, to which she was quick to respond with perfect good humour. She did not seem to be at all embarrassed about it but, by then in early adolescence and half understanding, I was.

Betty was a local girl, the daughter of a coalman who plied the neighbouring streets delivering coal with his horse and cart to families like ours. I suppose that, because of the pregnancy, he was told of his daughter's marriage only after the event (which was no doubt the reason why the celebratory booze-up that evening took place in Gran's front room with none of Betty's family present). In Mum's view, Betty was 'common'. She certainly spoke in a loud voice for a woman, and used words like 'bloody' or 'bleeding' almost as freely as the men. But she was good-natured, friendly and young and, after the baby was born, I went round quite often to visit this new branch of the family in their basement flat in a tall Victorian house a few streets away.

Bern's wife, Nel, was very different. She was not so good-looking as Betty, although her thick-lensed glasses which magnified her myopic eyes gave her a wistful, dreamy look. She was a soft-spoken woman whose brief and unhappy childhood had been passed in a Catholic orphanage in a remote part of Ireland. While still very young she had been sent into domestic service, and it was in one of her 'situations' that she had come to know Marjorie, who was to introduce her to Bern. Marjorie had married a friend of Bern's who lived next door to us, and after the marriage she had moved into the upstairs rooms of her in-laws' home just as Mum had done with Gran and Grandad years earlier. As soon as I met Nel, which was at the engagement party her friend Marjorie gave for her, I was charmed not only by her soft Irish voice but by the warmth of her interest in the family she was a year or so later to acquire by marriage. After the wedding (which Mum considered extravagantly showy and therefore to be as much condemned, though for the opposite reason, as Betty's perfunctory shotgun occasion) I was soon on visiting terms with Nel too.

It was too or three years before Nel had a baby, having waited until she and Bern had built up a comfortable home. By then, Betty was on the way to the third of the six children she was to produce with what Mum considered indecent rapidity. 'According to Betty, having babies is nothing,' she told me indignantly some years later. Whether this was true or not, as the new babies arrived, visits to Betty became less attractive to me. Good-natured and easygoing though she was, I preferred the warm attention – not to mention the dainty teas – that Nel offered.

Nel's second, and last, child was barely toddling when war broke out. At first unwilling to be separated from either Bern or the children, Nel stayed on in London until shortly before Bern volunteered for the Royal Engineers. For his peace of mind, as much as for the sake of the children, Nel agreed to go to the country, promising Bern she would stay there for the duration.

At first Bern was on the dangerous work of bomb disposal and, although Nel worried, while Bern remained in England it was not too bad because she had his leave to look forward to. But even before he was sent abroad, Nel was often lonely and the message soon got back to me that she and the children were longing for visitors, and that I should be specially welcome.

The idea of a weekend in the country was an attractive one to me, particularly after the air raids began, and it was arranged that for my first visit I should go with Nina, Nel's younger sister, so that she could show me how to get there. I knew Nina quite well. She had been chief bridesmaid at the wedding and she was often at Nel's when I called in because she and Nel were very close. They had shared their brief years of childhood in the same harsh orphanage, during which Nel had taken on the role of little mother to Nina. Of a more rebellious temperament than her sister, Nina hated the domestic service that had inevitably been her fate when she left the orphanage. She eagerly took the opportunity the war gave her and found a factory job in London, and lodgings a mere bus-ride away from her beloved sister. In the factory the hours were long, and the work was arduous, but to Nina it was a new and far happier life.

There was a Green Line bus which went from central London and passed through Colliers End, the village in Hertfordshire to which Nel and the children had been evacuated. When we got there I was thrilled to see that it really *was* a village, with weatherboard cottages of different shapes and sizes haphazardly ranged behind the high footpaths bordering each side of the road. The coach-stop was outside the Lamb, a large country pub set well back from the road, and as we got off Nina said, 'I expect they'll come to look for us as soon as they see the coach go by.' Sure enough, before it was out of sight we saw Nel and the two children emerging from a house that seemed to mark the end of the village.

'Well,' said Nel in her familiar soft and slightly breathless tones, 'you've got here!' She was smiling, and behind the thick lenses of her glasses her huge eyes seemed to express a childlike wonder. She was obviously as delighted at my being there as I was. 'The children are so excited,' she went on unnecessarily (as they were making it clear enough by their jumping and chattering). 'They've been talking all afternoon about seeing their "coz" again.' Nina, having hugged Nel, turned her attention to the children, accepting without rancour that for the moment Nel's main interest was in seeing me rather than her.

It took us only a minute to reach the end of the village and arrive at the Plough Inn, beyond which the road continued northwards through open country. The pub was a simple rectangular-shaped building, of which Nel's small part at one end had its own side entrance. The roof was of slate, not the prettily weathered red tiles of most of the cottages. Built of yellow brick (which at the pub end had been covered with plaster and a dingy, mushroom-coloured wash), it looked drab. As we walked through the rickety gate into the small bit of garden that had been fenced off round Nel's end of the dwelling it became clear to me that my expectation of a rural cottage was not to be fulfilled. Still, it was fun to find that it was next door to a real country pub, where a sign emblazoned in green and gold swung at the top of a wooden post.

Inside, the furnishings were minimal, which in one way was just as well because there was not much space. The front door opened straight into the living-room, most of which seemed to be taken up by a heavy old table and two or three upright wooden chairs. By the fireplace stood one battered armchair, and under the sash-window that looked on to the road was a small harmonium, which Nel said did not work. A door encrusted with dark green paint led to a scullery at the back where there was an old yellow sink and a cold-water tap, but no gas or electricity – cooking had to be done on a spirit stove. Another door with a lift-up latch shut off the dark and narrow staircase to the two bedrooms above.

That evening for supper we had huge, flat field mushrooms which we had found growing in starlike profusion in a nearby field. Nel fried them in dripping and served them on toast with a cup of her strong brew of tea to wash them down. After the children had been put to bed we lingered for a while at the table enjoying more tea and listening to the mounting sounds of talk and laughter coming through the party wall from the Plough. When the light faded Nel stood on a chair and lit the oil lamp which hung from the ceiling and then put a match to the fire. She said this was because 'there's always a chill in the air here in the evenings', but it was really to cast a more comfortable glow on the bare surroundings.

It was not long before Nina, tired from her long hours in the factory, began to yawn and then crept away upstairs. But comfortably settled each side of the fire, Nel in the armchair on one side while I was perched on the fender stool on the other, we were in less of a hurry to get to bed. Once past closing-time the noise from the Plough subsided, and soon only the crackle of the wood from the fire disturbed a quietness which Nel said was oppressive in the long evenings she was there on her own but which to me, after London, was a marvel.

Nel was eager to hear about what I had been up to, who I had been out with and, as ever, gently egged me on to tell her about my latest dreams and ambitions. I do not suppose that her harsh beginnings had encouraged her to have many ambitions of her own, although I have no doubt that she had plenty of dreams – like that of meeting someone she could love and be loved by, and above all marry. That this dream had come true was still, after nine years of marriage, a source of wonder to her, so that whatever bright future I hoped for had to include, in her eyes, marriage too. She was convinced, like everyone else who was older than I seemed to be, that I would swiftly change my negative attitude to marriage if the 'right man' came along. When it emerged that for several months I had been seeing a lot of someone with whom, I was willing to admit, I was quite besotted, Nel wanted to hear all I could tell her about him. And, despite my denials, the more she heard of Andrew, the more she expressed her conviction that this time it might be the man for me. By the end of the evening, when the fire had died down and midnight come and gone, we went upstairs – Nel to share her bed with Nina in the larger bedroom in which the children also slept, and I to sleep in the old and sagging double bed that almost filled the other small bedroom. We had agreed before we lifted the latch of the door to the stairs that next time I came to Colliers End I should bring Andrew too, if the romance was still thriving.

As the months went by my romance with Andrew continued to blow hot and cold, largely because of my unpredictable moods and flighty behaviour. I would not give up the freedom to go out with other men friends, such as Don, which must have caused Andrew as much misery as my recurrent attacks of discontent and despondency. It was one of these black moods that had led to my attempt to join the WAAF and resulted in my interview with Mr Iliffe. At about the same time, at the end of an evening with Andrew during which I had wrapped myself in un-approachable gloom, I suddenly decided to break off from him. In a way, I still believed I loved him, yet I knew I did not want to marry him and nor did I want to go on as before.

Some weeks later, coming home from work, I got into the train at London Bridge and found myself sitting next to David, the brother of my old school friend Sally, whose parents' home was in the same road as Andrew's. Not having heard of our quarrel, David asked me how Andrew was getting on, and from this the alarming news emerged that he had had a haemorrhage from the lungs and was in hospital with suspected tuberculosis. On arriving home, I broke down into sobs as I told Mum about it, and then wallowed in her quite undeserved sympathy. I suppose she saw my tears as remorse at my unreasonable treatment of such an acceptable suitor.

Next day I rushed off to the hospital, encouraged by Mum and Dad who by now looked on Andrew almost as a member of the family. In their eyes, he understood and loved their quixotic daughter as they did. In fact, they were well on the way to looking on him as their prospective son-in-law. In contrast, Andrew's parents – with some reason on their side – had not warmed to me any more than I had to them. I was frequently irritated by my parents' ways, which I considered unrefined, but I found Mr and Mrs Cooper's smug conventionalism even less acceptable. Invited to Sunday tea, I had managed to rouse Mrs Cooper, a plump and naturally placid woman, to such fury by arguing that wedding-rings were 'a stupid convention' that we were never really at ease with each other from then on.

When Andrew fell ill it was more than a year since we had first met in the upstairs kitchen in Lampmead Road. It was in those early days when we were still getting to know each other that I had realized that Andrew, despite his extra years, had less experience with the opposite sex than I had. I knew this from our first kiss on the front step. But he was quick to catch up. Before long our passionate embraces made me uneasily aware that we were getting into dangerous waters; for, in spite of my greater sophistication at kissing, I was still not so much innocent as ignorant about sex. It was not the possibility of losing my virginity that worried me. By now I had firmly discarded as conventional and outmoded the idea that this should be preserved until marriage. Such a notion was, I thought, inappropriate for a young woman like myself who had other dreams for the future than just finding a husband. What I did fear was getting pregnant. And the reason I feared it was not only because of the horror of 'having to get married' but also, and illogically, because of the shame of being found out at having indulged in sex before marriage!

Such worries, of course, did not cool our ardour, and our love-making continued in any odd corner we could find. In Lampmead Road the front porch was one obvious place, another the nearby local park where as a three-year-old I had fed the ducks and marvelled at the first sight of crocuses in spring. Because of the Blitz the great wrought-iron park gates were no longer locked at dusk, and a bench under one of the huge, ancient elms which looked down on the darkly shimmering lake was, on any fine night, a happily secluded haven. At weekends, when we had more time, we could spend hours in the bracken under the birch trees of a nearby wood which, although a bus-ride away, was not too far to walk home from if we lingered after dark.

Soon after Andrew's return home from hospital we spent an idyllic Sunday afternoon together in the woods, hidden in the bracken. Andrew suggested we should go back to his house for tea – an idea which did not seem at all attractive to me until he added that his parents had gone away for the weekend. In their sitting-room a newly erected Morrison shelter jutted out from the inside wall like a one-sided iron tent. It spoilt the look of the room, which was a quite pleasant one with its modern bay window, light paintwork, chintz-covered sofa and Chinese vases. Having made quite sure that the house was empty, we were soon locked together on the rose-and-beige patterned carpet. In the warm glow cast by the bars of an electric fire I opened my eyes to look at Andrew. His soft, dark hair was falling over one side of his forehead, his red lips glistening. Soon after, with a brief stab of pain, I knew that I was no longer a virgin. I had no regrets, but at the same time I knew that lying on the floor in a suburban house was not the romantic setting I had imagined and dreamt of for this auspicious moment.

A few weeks later I took Andrew with me to Colliers End. Nel was delighted to see us. She had already met Andrew who, at my suggestion, had called on her while working in nearby Letchworth, where his engineering firm had moved part of their works and where he was increasingly involved in the design of war weapons. This meant that some weeks Andrew and I saw each other only at weekends, which both diminished the hazards to our relationship caused by my moods and increased our ardour.

At Colliers End we went for a walk, played with the children and, after they had gone to bed, sat round the fire talking with Nel until, around midnight, she announced that she was going to bed. 'If you are coming into *my* bed, Phyll,' she said in her usual quiet tone of voice, 'don't make a noise and disturb the children.' Her eyes looked more myopic than usual behind the thick lenses, and her lips quivered with a conspiratorial smile. 'Good-night,' she said, and looking pointedly at Andrew, 'Now be careful!' Without saying anything explicitly, we knew that she knew; and I knew that she (and probably Andrew as well) believed that I was now surely started on the well-worn route to marriage, even if I was not yet officially engaged. As an aberrant but deeply convinced Catholic, she believed that God would look with a more merciful eye upon human passion than the priests she knew did – so long as it was in good faith!

At little later, Andrew and I crept up the dark wooden stairs to our bedroom. The light of the candle threw long patterns of shadows and light which flickered on white walls and ceiling and gleamed on the brass knobs of the bedstead. It was cold, but in our delight we hardly noticed as, between hugs and kisses, we tussled with our clothes. Andrew blew out the candle and pulled back the curtains before jumping into bed beside me. I was wearing pyjamas Mum had made me from a remnant of shirt material of mauve stripes, but in the light of the moon everything was drained of its colour and turned magically silver. The hoot of an owl and the groan of the pub sign as it swayed in the wind added to the enchantment.

A week later we set off together for a holiday in South Devon. Our landlady could not be expected to be as helpfully broad-minded as Nel, and as an unmarried pair we were naturally given separate rooms. We were much too uncertain of ourselves to ask for anything else, or even to make any clandestine visits to each other's rooms during the night. Our more passionate moments had to be found on the moors and grassy banks of Devon which, in the lovely spring weather, had its own special magic.

Every day after a substantial cooked breakfast we set off to explore the area, finding a sandwich for lunch where we could, sometimes in neighbouring Dorset. At Lyme Regis, whose cliff-hanging structure seemed thrillingly foreign to me, we sat with our feet hanging over the sea wall eating cream cakes of a kind no longer to be found in wartime London. In the evening, back at our lodgings, the landlady provided another substantial meal that owed little to the ration books we had handed over to her. After our supper we invariably took another leisurely stroll around nearby lanes, and one evening we paid a visit to the local clairvoyant. The air was scented with the smell of the primroses and violets flowering in abundance on the high banks as we pranced gaily along in the twilight, and the moon and the stars were already shining brilliantly. The sky was not yet black, but it was dark enough to make weird silhouettes of the small twisted oak trees that lined the lane.

Just beyond the edge of the village Madam Dora, the clair-voyant, lived in an isolated dwelling which in the half-light looked more of a hut than a house. We were surprised to find ourselves invited into a tastefully furnished room in which there were comfortable armchairs, well-filled bookshelves and a highly polished old table on which stood a large bowl of primroses. A second surprise was that Madam Dora did not, as we had expected, pry for information before beginning to do her turn on each of us. After just a keen glance, she began on our characters – which did tend to be suspiciously flattering. I was 'proud, independent, artistic and fond of beautiful things', and Andrew was 'sensitive, artistic and introspective', all attributes to which we either aspired or were well content to accept! Her predictions for the future were more inspired. Far from assuming that we were a courting couple on the road to matrimony, which is what I expected, she said that I should be engaged before the end of the year to someone named Stephen. As I knew no one of that name, this sounded unlikely. And when she went on to say that my health would be under threat within a year or two, I wondered how she could be so misguided, since I looked the picture of health. I wondered even more what she could possibly now say to Andrew, who was waiting his turn beside me, and really did still look frail from his recent illness.

When Madam Dora got on to Andrew there were yet more surprises, the first being that she did not mention his health at all. Nor did she hold out much hope of a new romance on the near horizon for him, as she had done for me. This seemed to me a bit hard, since having predicted an end of our romance and a beginning of a new one for me, I felt she ought to have presented a replacement of me to him! On the contrary, she told Andrew that his immediate future would involve more work and study than love and – what must have been no consolation then to him – that in time he would marry a slim, fair-haired girl!

It was a just as well that we retained the same spirit of scepticism with which we had arrived, and left believing our seance with the clairvoyant to be no more than an amusing end to a beautiful day. As we strolled back to our lodgings, we ruminated over whether Madam Dora really believed that she had psychic powers, which in spite of the mysteriously atmospheric Devon night we were confident she did not. I was to discover later how large a part of her predictions were to be proved either accurate or very nearly so. But maybe it was her judgement of character, more than her predictive powers, that were the basis on which she built.

10
Meg's Decision

My visit to Andrew in hospital had reawakened my school-day
dreams of being a nurse. I was impressed particularly by the
charm of the young VAD who handed Andrew his tea while I
was there. It was the uniform again, this time the red cross on
the white overall, which re-evoked visions of my caring tenderly
for the sick and wounded (just as Mum and Vera Brittain had
done in their young days in the First World War). I was bored
with being an air-raid warden, which in my case had never
amounted to much; by some quirk of fate the times when I was
on duty were usually uneventful. I became more and more
dilatory in turning up at the wardens' post even though, once
we had moved, it was right next door, in a prefabricated hut
that had been erected in front of the ruins of the bombed school.
Partly because it was so close, and partly because I so hated
leaving my warm bed, I began to delay getting up when a
warning came and I was on duty. If there were signs of real
activity, such as the sound of aircraft or of guns firing, I knew
that I could be out of bed and round to the post within minutes.
But for many weeks nothing at all had happened between the
warning siren and the all-clear. I do not think my defaulting
ways mattered much. There was a core of keen and active
wardens for whom Civil Defence duty had become a way of
life. These men and women, whether on duty or not, spent
almost all their free time at the wardens' post and, unlike me,
carried out their duties more than conscientiously. Most of the
wardens were of youngish middle age and found it an enjoy-
able meeting-place, a kind of social club. For me it was
less interesting, as most of the young men who had not
volunteered or been conscripted into the forces preferred,
like Wal, Pete and Andrew, to join the Home Guard or

other auxiliary services such as the police or the fire service.

At this time I was still keenly attending lectures at Morley College, and it was there I discovered that a concentrated course for VADs was to start at the Westminster Division of the British Red Cross Society. I went along and found myself one of a small group of about a dozen young women. The lecturer was a dazzlingly attractive and petite blonde, whose looks were further enhanced by her commandant's uniform – a neat, navy blue suit and a matching brimmed felt hat with a fan-shaped cockade on one side.

As with most of my new starts, I launched myself into the course with enthusiasm, which meant that whenever a volunteer was called for I rushed forward. I do not suppose this worried the commandant, but it intrigued one member of the group who thought I was either objectionably pushy or enviably self-confident. She decided to speak to me to find out which. On discovering that I was a year older than she was, Meg Barrett fortunately decided on the more favourable interpretation. Long-legged and slimly built, Meg had light brown hair which she coaxed into loose, fluffy waves and curls, a square-shaped face with high cheek-bones, and grey eyes strangely speckled with brown. She wore no make-up and was distinctly pretty in a healthy-looking, natural way.

Meg and I quickly found we had much in common. Like me, Meg had been a 'scholarship girl' at a grammar school, now worked as a clerk in the City (though in an insurance company, not a bank), and seemed to come from a family much like mine, although from a different part of London. Apart from our similar backgrounds, we also had the same political sympathies (vaguely defined though these were); but above all we shared an aching ambition to 'travel', which we fed by much vicarious reading. Our own travels, largely restricted to the top deck of buses, were often enhanced by our earnest exchanges about the travel books we had currently borrowed from our local libraries.

Besides our dreams of travelling, we had at least two other favourite subjects. One was whether we should ever manage to escape from our boring jobs, preferably into an excitingly adventurous life to do with the war somewhere overseas. Another was our families. When we got round to visiting each other's homes, as we soon did, Meg and I knew even more surely how much common ground we shared. We both felt that our parents – more especially our mothers – had many failings, and these we often discussed. What we did not talk about yet instinctively recognized was that, despite our expressed discontent, both of us were more closely bound to our families than we were prepared to admit.

Meg's family lived at Ilford. Her father was a skilled worker at Ford's. He was a small, dark man with a marked Lancashire accent and a slight squint. Mrs Barrett, partly because of her solid build and upright bearing, looked a good deal larger than her husband. She had light brown hair, and a delightful slow and soft-toned voice with a Norfolk accent. But her face often had an almost dour expression – until she spoke, when it lightened into something like resigned placidity. The Barretts' home was more sparsely furnished than ours was (after our move, at any rate). Instead of the carpet square that we had, there was only lino on the living-room floor, with no more than a rag mat in front of the fire to cover the bareness. The Barretts were buying their house, and no doubt this left little over for other things. They could of course have used Mum's solution of buying on 'easy terms', but there was no evidence of their doing so, and I suspect that it was a solution of which Mrs Barrett would not have approved.

Like Mum's and Mrs Pluck's, and that of so many other women who had reared their families in the depressed inter-war years, Mrs Barrett's married life had not been an easy one. But although Mum and Dad had rows, they enjoyed life together; and despite her many complaints about him, Mum in some ways looked up to Dad. This was different from Meg's mother, who gave one the impression that she did not think much of her husband, or perhaps any men, except her two sons. Mrs Barrett had given birth to six children – two sons and four girls, of whom Meg was the first daughter. But tragedy had come for Mrs Barrett when the last of her children, twin girls, had died of pneumonia within hours of each other while they were still babies. Meg was about nine years old when this happened and deeply attached to the twins, whom she had helped to care for. She was desolated as much by her mother's inconsolable grief as her own. I think this was the reason that Meg, although just as often resentful of Mrs Barrett's moods or demands as I was of Mum's, usually deferred to her mother in a way I did not to mine. There was no doubt in my mind that Meg's mother was much more demanding. Meg was expected to help a lot with household chores like cleaning, while I did practically nothing for Mum. Similarly, when Meg came to our house for tea, it was Mum who willingly rushed around beforehand to make sure there was a suitable spread. One reason was that Meg, unlike some of the 'toffee-nosed' friends of my grammar-school days, was a popular guest, welcomed by Dad and my brothers as well, if they happened to be around. At the Barretts' the conversation was often lively, especially if Meg's sister or elder brother were there. But the food was not lavish – and it was Meg's job to get it. Mrs Barrett always seemed to be weary, and the most she would do was to agree that a boiled egg might be spared, or to offer other instructions, while meanwhile she lolled back in her chair by the fire.

By the time the course at Westminster had ended, the friendship between Meg and me was firmly established. We began to talk about joining up together as VADs, but first we had to complete our training by doing fifty hours of practical work in a hospital. As this had to be fitted in after work – that is, in evenings or at weekends – we each went to hospitals near our homes. I arranged to go to St John's, a small voluntary hospital about a mile and a half away from Lee and easy to get to by tram.

As I walked up the hill in the dark towards the entrance to the hospital on the first evening I was so frightened that I longed to run away. 'If you can only make yourself do this,' I told myself desperately, 'you will know that you can make yourself do anything.' For a while I continued to feel frightened as I approached the hospital, but once inside and as I was putting on the blue dress and crisp white apron with its large red cross on the bib, I felt braver.

I very much enjoyed wafting about the wards smiling cheerfully and speaking kindly to patients – this was the image of nursing I had cherished for years. As a mere trainee VAD the chores I had to do were less attractive, being largely menial tasks such as fetching and carrying jugs of water or the evening drinks, and helping with bedpan rounds. All the same, as patients got to know me, it was good to be greeted so warmly by them when I appeared in the wards. 'It's always a pleasure to see your rosy cheeks and smiling face. It cheers you up,' said one flaccid-faced, middle-aged woman. At that time sick people stayed in hospital for much longer periods, often remaining for weeks, if not months, rather than days; and wards had a quite different atmosphere – and also a quite different smell. There was always the pungent odour of sickness, suppuration and boiling of instruments struggling against the strong smell of disinfectant.

On most of my evenings I came under the wing of Staff Nurse White. She had a face that was pleasant-looking as well as pretty. Her dark brown eyes and high-coloured cheeks were striking, as was the unusual dent – almost a dimple – at the end of her well-shaped nose. Unless she was very pressed, she took me along with her when she went on her treatment rounds, and gave me simple tasks to do like holding the bowl for discarded dressings. I was often appalled at the ugly, oozing wounds I saw and by the moaning, pasty-faced – no longer quite human – creatures suffering from them. On one occasion I stood by while she dressed the wound of a poor old man who had what looked like a small lidded casserole inserted in his belly. Underneath the lid was a yawning wound which Nurse White had to clean. I wondered if I might faint, and remembered how as a child Mum had mocked me when I went home crying from some slight graze from a fall in the street. 'I don't know what you'd do if you went to hospital. You'd die of fright!' I did not die, or even faint, but by the time I had done my fifty hours I was not quite so sure that I wanted to became a full-time VAD.

This did not stop me from being furious with Meg when I heard that she had not waited for me to make up my mind and had enrolled without me. But when I had recovered from my bad temper I was eager to learn how she was getting on. By good luck she was posted to the military hospital, the Royal Herbert, at Woolwich. As this was only another short tram-ride away from Lee, we were able to continue seeing each other. Many of my friendships were to be broken by the war, but this one was to last a lifetime.

After further dithering, I decided that the life of a VAD was
not for me. But at last events were conspiring to bring about the
changes in my life that I so desired but had not the courage to
make happen. The demands of the war were spreading the
conscription net wider. Wal had been called up months ago,
and Pete was about to follow him. A government committee set
up to examine the man- and woman-power needs of the war
had concluded that some of the 'reserved occupations' must be
squeezed again to release more recruits. The National Provincial Bank was amongst those which had to lose several hundred
more staff, and for the first time including some women. Even
so there were only three women who were allowed to go from
the bank's head office, of whom I was one and Pluckie another.
As a pacifist Pluckie would not consider joining anything
remotely connected with the armed forces, but decided that she
would accept conscription into the Land Army.

Although afraid that waiting until I was conscripted might
mean I should end up in the ATS, which I thought the least
appealing of the women's services, I was relieved that at last I
was going to be plucked out of banking and not therefore
doomed to spend the entire war in a quiet backwater (which, in
spite of the Blitz, I quite wrongly continued to believe London
to be). It was also a relief that I no longer had to worry about
upsetting Mum and Dad, who accepted conscription as an
unavoidable necessity and different from leaving home of one's
own volition. Best of all, as a permanent member of the bank
staff, I should get my service pay made up to my normal salary
by the bank. This meant that I should be getting a useful
supplement to the few shillings a week that I should get in the
services. I should also be able to go on giving Mum something
towards the household expenses with little cost to myself.

However, as a woman, there was one way in which I could
still avoid being conscripted. That was to get married. I knew
that Andrew was willing, and sometimes during our best
moments together I thought I might be too. Then I would draw
back – for, to me, marriage continued to seem like the end of the
road; and if that was where I was doomed to end up eventually
(which by now I was more inclined to think I might be), I still
believed that to get there at the age of twenty was too soon!
Surprisingly, much as they liked Andrew, Mum and Dad did

nothing to press me into marriage, even though that would have kept me close to them.

Once or twice that autumn Andrew and I went down together to Colliers End. We picked mushrooms and black-berries, and looked after the children one evening while Nel went to a whist drive. Andrew, without much success, tried to play the harmonium to amuse the children, and after we had put them to bed he washed my hair in rainwater from the butt outside the door. But in spite of oil lamp and candle-light and the creaking sign swinging in the wind outside, the magic of it all was not quite as it had been during our first visit. Andrew seemed to have lost some of the endearing mad humour that had first drawn me to him, and to be almost oppressed by his work. With some reason, he was also depressed and apprehensive about the future.

For one thing, I was up to my old tricks again. Another of the young men who had disappeared into the services reappeared one day by the side of my ledger. It was the young man whose invitation I had turned down a few months after I had started work at the bank because I did not like his red hair and arrogant manner. Now he had turned up again unexpectedly, rather as Don Faversham had done, after many months in the United States, where he had been sent to train as a pilot. The combi-nation of the glamour of his uniform and his travels was irresistible to me – and he was called Stephen, the very name Madam Dora had conjured up in Devon! If anything, this time my behaviour was worse than ever. I told Andrew all about Stephen, but I told Stephen very little about Andrew. For although I was flattered by the fact that after all these months, and all his enviable adventures, Stephen clearly still had me on his mind, I did not mean to take him seriously. I did, however, convince myself that it was more or less a patriotic duty to help him to enjoy his leave.

For once, Pluckie was nearly as exasperated by my flightiness as Andrew. She felt she had seen enough of Stephen at the bank to form an opinion of him, and she believed that I could not possibly have as much in common with him as I had with Andrew. He was politically conservative, class-conscious, and in many ways far too conventional for me, she said, especially in his attitudes towards women. I knew all this was true, and also that there was in him a hardness and a will to dominate which, though it fascinated me, at the same time made me uneasy. However, Stephen was willing to accept that our relationship must for the time being remain platonic, and indeed this fitted in perfectly well with his conventional approach to courting a pure young woman, which he evidently presumed I was. At the end of his leave we promised to keep in touch; but, as he had forewarned me, his letters were matter-of-fact and dull, lacking any of the attraction he had when he was present.

Over the following winter months my duplicity continued. Andrew remained my lover but had to put up with my temporary desertion each time Stephen appeared on leave. I was often uneasy about my capricious behaviour but unable to control it, and it must have been even harder for poor Andrew to understand. Permeating everything was our awareness that, in any event, we must soon be separated. At the beginning of March 1943 I was called for a medical examination, soon after which I was accepted for service in the WAAF. Now that the die was cast, Andrew did his best to conceal his misery by joining with Mum, Dad and Joe in jokes about how I should be likely to get on. Impressed by the pictures I had seen in the recruitment literature of girls in battledress working on fighter aircraft, I let out that, if I had the chance, I hoped to be a flight mechanic. Dad's thin lips twisted into one of his familiar expressions. Quizzical and shrewd, his blue eyes glinting humorously, he said, 'That won't suit you, girl! You'll be out in all weathers, your nails will always be broken, and your hands will be so grimed with dirt they'll never be clean.' Of course I vehemently rejected the suggestion that I was much too soft and fussy to put up with such things – but I was disconcerted.

Andrew came to see me off on a train bound for Gloucester a fortnight later. I felt keyed up and very nervous, but I did not regret that I was going. It was three and a half years since the war had begun and at last my dreams of an adventurous new life were, I hoped, about to come true.

11
Taking Off

The first days were a shock. It was bewildering to be immersed in a throng of new recruits and to be herded from place to place, waiting around to be issued with uniform and other equipment, and being given numerous 'preliminary instructions'. The feeling of having been suddenly stripped of one's identity was made worse by one's being almost completely cut off from the life one had left behind. For at first no incoming post was allowed, and the only way to get in touch with home was to wait one's turn at the end of a long queue to make a brief telephone call from one of the few kiosks to be found near the guarded entrance.

At the end of the first day I got thankfully into my bed, which was about half-way along the prefabricated hut I shared with another twenty-nine new recruits, and I found it hard not to weep as the mournful sound of last post wailed through Tannoy speakers at each end of the hut. I woke with a heavy heart at six o'clock next morning to the more bracing, but equally unwelcome, noise of reveille. It was several days before it dawned on me that the overwhelming sense of misery, which seemed to make my whole body ache, was not that I was sickening for something but an acute attack of homesickness.

Yet by the end of the first week I had begun to enjoy the healthy open-air life, which seemed so much more agreeable than being shut up all day in a City office. I also enjoyed the camaraderie of the other girl recruits, who were the more interesting because many came from, to me, unknown parts of the country like Scotland, and even far-away parts of the world like Iceland, Jamaica and Canada. However, my unaccustomed neck was rubbed sore by the stiff collars of shirts and greatcoat, and breaking in the heavy black shoes on route marches and 'square-bashing' was agonizing. But although the inoculations made me feel ill, nothing was quite as bad as I feared it might be. The regimentation was real enough, but the emphasis was on activity and interest, not heavy-handed discipline. Nor was it all drill and marching. The attractive young WAAF officers who gave us lectures on subjects ranging from hygiene to politics held our attention through their own enthusiasm. Even the fatigues were far from onerous – although enough to give me pause for the first time to ponder the lightness of my share of chores at home.

In spite of my having scoffed at his comments, Dad had in fact impressed me enough over the disadvantages of being a flight mechanic to make me think again. When the time came for the trade test to sort out who could do what, I put down for training as a meteorological observer. Watching the weather sounded a pleasant kind of job, even if less dramatic than that of flight mechanic. After being accepted for this, I was overjoyed to discover that one of the training courses for this 'trade' was based in London. It would mean six whole weeks during which I would be able to get home, and also see Andrew. The attraction of both had been quickened again by the short, sharp shock of my enforced separation from them. In addition, it would mean that I could be in London for my twenty-first birthday.

I returned to a billet in Chelsea, in a large block of red-brick Edwardian flats requisitioned to house WAAF personnel for the duration. It was an easy walk to Victoria Station, from where I could pick up a tram that would take me to Lee in the evenings and at weekends, and it was on the Sunday following my birthday that I went home to celebrate it. The familiar Sunday morning smell of roasting meat and baking pastry greeted me when I arrived. I knew that for this occasion we were to have one of the chickens that Dad now had scratching about up the yard, portions of which would be served up on plates, which I would have to bring in, one by one, from the kitchen, piled high with Mum's soggy greens and roast potatoes, and awash with gravy. Andrew was already there, and so was Joe, but I had to wait for my presents until Dad came back from the pub. Mum told me proudly he had found something special for me and wanted to be there to 'see my face'. He arrived home in bantering mood after his morning drinking, and handed over my present with a beery kiss. I was disappointed to find that it was only a long string of pale coral, neither new nor fashionable. I did my best to conceal my feelings because I knew of the time and trouble Dad had taken to find something that he thought would satisfy my 'arty' taste. Joe, on behalf of himself and Wal (who could not get leave from his anti-aircraft battery somewhere remote in south-west England), had a silver cigarette-case for me. This did please me, for although I seldom smoked, I should enjoy offering cigarettes to others from such an elegant case. Andrew's present was a new wrist-watch. This made me feel pretty mean because Stephen had written to say he was coming on leave and, once again, I was about to relegate Andrew to the sideline of friendship.

By this time Stephen was on his first tour of duty as a fighter pilot. Delighted with his lot, he took me out to lunch to celebrate and, it turned out, to propose we should get engaged. Bowled over by his dash and verve, I accepted. That night in bed in the room I shared with four other WAAFs, I buried my head under the sheet. It was the only way of ignoring the mice that ran everywhere – including over the beds – because, our superiors insisted, girls *would* bring food into the rooms. It was also the only way for me to escape the chatter of my companions so that I could worry about what I had done. How, I asked myself, had I got into this situation of being engaged to Stephen, whom I hardly knew and had barely kissed, when as a result of our passionate reunion a few weeks earlier I could possibly be pregnant by Andrew?

When Andrew went round to tell Mum and Dad about the engagement they were as much dismayed by his distress as by my behaviour. Mum told him to try not to worry – 'she'll come to her senses before long' – and the following Sunday told me that I did not deserve 'a decent fellow like he is'. This was no more than I had expected, but I was astonished to find that Dad felt he had to tackle me too. He managed to do so by catching me in the yard where I had wandered up to see Dizzy in order to escape from the disapproving atmosphere in the living-room. Mum had been too het up to mince words about what she rightly considered my utterly selfish behaviour; Dad's approach was to try friendly mateyness. 'What's all this about this Stephen, then?' he began.

I tried awkwardly to respond in the same manner. 'Oh, I don't know, Dad. It's no good talking about, it, really. I've got engaged, and that's it.'

'But what do you mean, "engaged"? Is it a ring you want? If you want a ring, Andrew will get you one. You know he would! You know he'd walk a mile to buy you a bar of chocolate!'

As I had always been so contemptuous of the notion of 'getting engaged', this touched a raw spot, and I indignantly denied that 'wanting a ring' had anything to do with it.

The ring Stephen had bought me was a pretty flower-shaped cluster of small diamonds round a garnet centre. We had chosen it together at a jewellers in Oxford Street and it cost £30. Invited to lunch to meet his parents and celebrate the occasion, I displayed the ring. But Stephen's father, Stephen told me later, was angry about it. The diamonds were of poor quality, he had said, and a far better ring for the same amount could have been bought through his business contacts. I remembered my quarrel with Andrew's mother; although I had now changed my mind and accepted the convention of rings, something was apparently still not right. The question of rings, I decided, was a tricky area in the world of conventional suburbia; a world in which I still felt ill at ease.

I was glad to escape again from London and, fully fledged after the six weeks' training, eager to find out what life as a meteorological observer would offer. I was posted to RAF Station Woolfox Lodge, an airfield in Rutland where bomber aircrews completed their training before going on to their first tour of operations. A few miles north of Stamford the station straddled the main road to Peterborough. On the perimeter of the airfield, about a mile to the east of the road, stood the control tower. The Met Office, which I was about to join, was on the ground floor of this square concrete building of two floors. The rest of the station, where the stores and living quarters were based, was on the other side of the main road. Nissen huts for the WAAFs had been set up in a field in a far corner of the camp. The field sloped down to a beautiful lake surrounded by chestnut trees.

Although at first I felt as if I were miles from anywhere, and really out in the wilds, I soon learnt how easy it was to get away from the camp and into Stamford or farther afield. Even with petrol rationing, there was a flow of traffic on the trunk road beside Woolfox Lodge, and one seldom had to wait long before someone stopped to offer a lift. Not that I had any objection to staying in the camp for much of the time, for there was a happy atmosphere there and there were plenty of social activities. Issued on arrival with a bicycle, I soon settled to a way of life where taking a bath meant blithely cycling round the edge of a field with a greatcoat over one's pyjamas to reach the bath-hut, and going on and off duty meant windswept cycle-rides across the airfield to get to the Met Office.

For the first time since I had left school five years earlier I had a job I liked and believed to be suited to my abilities. Both the work and the surroundings were wonderfully different from anything I had known before. The Met Office had windows on three sides with distant views under panoramic skies. Here throughout the day and night the weather in all its variations had to be observed, plotted and reported on; one of my duties as a 'Met girl' was to go outside every ten minutes to the hour every hour to take readings of barometric pressure, temperature and rainfall, as well as to assess visibility, wind direction and force, and type and amount of cloud. All over the country at several hundred stations WAAFs like me (and, on some naval stations, Wrens) were following exactly the same procedure at exactly the same time each hour of the day and the night. Every 'observation' had to be sent through to higher levels in coded form on a teleprinter. All these coded details sent in from every station were relayed by the teleprinter back to everyone, and were used for drawing up the meteorological maps on which forecasts were based.

At Woolfox Lodge there were two 'forecasters', former career meteorologists from the Civil Service who had only recently been taken into the RAF as uniformed officers, who were assisted by WAAF meteorological observers. The forecasting of weather was, as their title implied, the job of the two scientific officers, not of 'trade' WAAFs, such as I was, whose more modest task was to make the hourly observations and do the elementary work on the maps. At that time, of course, forecasting lacked today's advanced technology and was even less of an exact science. So that although taken seriously in the planning of flying operations, forecasting was the butt of a good deal of derisive comments. Even so the Met Office, apart from the real service it afforded aircrew, was a popular place, not only for weather predictions (which could be as much of a threat to plans for evening outings as to flying) but for the attractions of cups of coffee and tea, and the company that went with them.

Flying Officer Hatcher, known to all as 'Hatch', the forecaster in charge, was an amiable, easygoing fellow whose most remarkable feature was a large, dark and drooping moustache. He did not seem to mind having the office turned into a social club so long as the work was carried out efficiently and well, which he knew that Maureen, his senior WAAF, would ensure. Maureen was younger than I was but already a corporal. She was a tall, carefree girl of nineteen, with an attractive snub nose, small bright eyes, a fresh complexion sprinkled with freckles, and the ebullience of a Labrador puppy. It was her job to arrange the duty rota, and it was typical of her unaffected ways that she did not exclude herself from night duty, although as a corporal she could have done.

When the flying stopped, so did almost everything else, leaving the Met WAAF on duty feeling very much alone in the vast and eerie emptiness of the darkened airfield. The forecaster went home to his bed, while upstairs in the control tower the one or two left on duty in case of emergency tucked down to sleep. It was not so bad in the summer; even with the 'double summer time' of the war the first streaks of dawn could be seen above the eastern horizon soon after three in the morning. But as winter approached, to fumble through dense fog to find the instrument box, or have to go out into the darkness when owls were screeching or, worst of all, to find a crowd of rats scuffling round dustbins, was no fun. When it was time to go outside and the rats seemed more threatening than usual, I climbed through the window to avoid them. Between observations there were maps to draw up, cups of coffee to be made to fight off dozing, letters to write and books to read, but even so the nights often seemed very long.

It was no fun either trying to sleep in the daytime. In a Nissen hut shared with so many others I never had any difficulty in going to sleep when I wanted to as long as it was around normal bedtime. But it was a very different matter when one tried to tuck down in daytime. Almost always some girls were having a day off, or getting up late, or lighting or stoking up the small, round stove that kept us warm. It was hard to get even an hour or two of unbroken sleep, and one frequently got up feeling as bleary-eyed as when one had got into the narrow bed with its thin mattress made up of three squares called 'biscuits'. It was a hardship that had to be set against the advantages of shift work, which included rest days (tacked on to leave, they could extend it) and, above all, the sense of freedom one had from a boring, unchanging routine.

Considering how little privacy there was in the huts and how mixed were the groups occupying them, I was surprised to find how easy it was to fit into this communal life. Of course there were clashes and girls one did not like. But it seemed that, if one had to, one could learn to get on with – or at any rate tolerate – almost anyone. Then again, and perhaps because almost all women start early to practise the skills of home-making, there was seldom any problem about keeping the hut clean; and many chores got done on the basis of volunteering for what one liked best – or disliked least. I liked to be warm, so I always aimed to get a bed near the centre of the hut and close to the stove, but this meant taking on the job of tidying up round it and seeing that it was kept alight, although I was as reluctant as everyone else to volunteer to chop wood or fill up the coal-bucket. Likewise, it was usually the shyer or more reserved girl who chose a bed in a corner nearest the door, and this was often the same kind of person who woke early and would take on the responsibility of warning others that it was time to get up.

Every hut had WAAFs from a mixture of 'trades' – drivers, cooks and clerks, and many more. There were five of us Met girls. We were on friendly terms with all the others in our hut, but we quickly became more of a close coterie. Apart from Maureen, there was Jess from the Midlands, a languorous, soft-spoken girl with green eyes. When she woke in the mornings she looked like a washed-out rag doll, but with make-up on and her light brown hair teased out like spun sugar she had a burnished glamour that somehow contrived to make even her uniform look better than anyone else's. She was specially friendly with Jean, who had bouncy dark hair and beautiful blue eyes, and a habit of cocking her head slightly to one side and pouting a little when seeking a favour. Most men found this mannerism irresistible, and she used it to good effect for getting us things like extra tea or coffee from the station's stores.

And then there was Tony. She was small and full-breasted with slightly protruding front teeth, a perky smile and heavy golden hair which she wore like Veronica Lake, the film star, in a long page-boy style. It attracted all eyes – including the ever watchful ones of the administrative WAAF officers concerned to keep hair, as prescribed by regulations, at or above collar-level. Tony was the daughter of a Chelmsford solicitor, and she and her family had some strange ways, or so it seemed to me at that time. The family were nature lovers, and early and peace-able converts to the cause of animal rights. For a while we had trouble in the hut persuading Tony that she could not keep a field-mouse she had found in her suitcase as a pet. An even stranger predilection of hers in my eyes was that she felt all clothes to be constraining. When at home, she told me, she often walked about the house naked, which both she and her parents considered perfectly natural. These extraordinary parents, I found on meeting them later, looked disappointingly old, shrivelled and mild compared with my own. There was one way in which Tony had followed convention: on the third finger of her left hand she wore a plain diamond ring. She was engaged to a soldier who fought at El Alamein and who was still somewhere abroad on active service. Tony's courtship had been even more rapid than mine with Stephen. She had met Sonny only days before the end of his embarkation leave and had not seen him since. After more than a year's separation, and able to keep in touch only through letters, she did not doubt their love but had anguished moods when she feared that Sonny would never return. Such an attractive girl, in a camp where men outnumbered women by at least ten to one, was not short of admirers; but she always made clear before accepting any invitation that she was irretrievably committed elsewhere. It was a long time before Sonny was to return, but when he did so they got married almost as quickly – and with the same confidence – as they had got engaged.

My engagement proved to be less enduring. I had not been long at Woolfox Lodge before a telegram came to say that

Stephen had crashed. Pulled out of his burning aircraft, with severe burns to one of his legs, he spent six suffering months in hospital, facing painful skin-grafts, and fears of permanent disablement and its effect on his – and our – future. On my first visit to him, he suggested we should end our engagement; but out of a sense either of loyalty or of romantic drama, maybe a bit of both, I would not agree to this. Luckily Stephen recovered completely and was able to return to flying, but by then whatever it was that had drawn us together was waning. Perhaps because of Stephen's respect for my presumed purity, and my guilt about my affair with Andrew, our love-making had never gone beyond a few awkward kisses. The spark of physical passion was missing. We parted on unfriendly terms – and to my shame I had to be prompted to return that trouble-some ring. The damage was, I think, only to Stephen's pride, and on my side an uneasy conscience. But at least I had learnt a lesson from the experience and determined never to put myself in the same false position again.

One reason for the happy atmosphere at Woolfox Lodge was that the commanding officer, a young group captain, was more of a democrat than a disciplinarian. He also had a sense of humour – or so it seemed to me from the wry expression on his face when, eight months after arriving at Woolfox Lodge, I stood at attention in front of him on a charge of being absent without leave. A fortnight earlier at the behest of higher and unknown authorities the Met Office was closed down. The forecasters were promptly posted elsewhere and we Met WAAFs were left to await instructions. Tony was the first to go. She disappeared into remote, inaccessible West Suffolk. I added her name to my growing list of dispersed correspondents, and from then on we met only on the rare occasions when our leave coincided.

The Met Office having closed, those of us left had no work to do. The first few days were very pleasant. We got up late, cycled round the field to take leisurely baths, took country walks in the spring sunshine, and spent days hitch-hiking to places of historical interest in the area. After a week of this kind of activity we began to get bored, but by then the administrative 'bods' had got wind of us and started closing in. We were given the job of picking up rubbish round the camp, which seemed a

demeaning and undeserved task. When a further order reached
us to report for another job Maureen and I decided to ignore it,
partly because we had already made plans to hitch-hike to
Peterborough to meet two American servicemen we had got to
know there.

It was at the end of the day in Peterborough that we
impulsively decided to get a train to London instead of returning to camp. I told Maureen that she could come home with me,
because she said her parents would be upset and angry over
what we were planning to do. I had no fears that Mum and
Dad would react like that. I remembered too clearly the stories
I had heard as a child of the times in the Great War when Dad
had temporarily cocked a snook at authority and gone home on
unofficial leave. I knew that, as a result, on one occasion he had
ended up imprisoned in Dover Castle, but I was fairly sure that
something less Draconian would happen to us.

Mum and Dad, as I expected, were not at all disconcerted
when we arrived home late that night, but they were concerned
that if we stayed too long the Military Police might arrive to
collect us. This would have been an ignominious end to our
defiance, so we went off next day to Colliers End. I don't know
what Mum or Dad told the police when they did come, but it
certainly would not have been where we had gone. When we got
to Nel's and explained why we had come she chided us in her
gentle way, and made clear that she thought our behaviour
foolish and rather wild. I had not seen her since I had become a
WAAF, but she had heard about my engagement. Although
not a word was exchanged between us, I knew that she
disapproved of this too, and that she felt I had betrayed her as
much as Andrew. This did not prevent her from taking us in
and, indeed, making us welcome. Family loyalty came first.

Two days later Maureen and I hitch-hiked back to Woolfox
Lodge. We had to appear before the chief WAAF officer to be
formerly charged and then remanded to appear next day before
the commanding officer. Marched in under escort to face the
group captain (with whom not long before I had been playing
in a mixed game of hockey at a nearby fighter station), I was
more amazed than abashed by the formality of the proceedings
which, under regulations, had to be scrupulously followed. It
was then that I noticed the group captain's wry expression. My

sentence was fourteen days confined to camp, and Maureen's a severe reprimand. But before my time was up our postings had come through. We were on our way to fields and pastures new.

12
Norfolk Days

I left Woolfox Lodge exactly ten months after joining up. In that time I had learnt that although there were some regulations in the RAF which could usually be safely ignored, amongst those which could not be were the dreadful procedures known as 'arriving' and 'clearing' a station. I could see that, when I was posted, it was important that I should hand my bicycle back to the section of the camp from which I had taken it on arrival. I could also see that a visit to the sick-bay to check that one had not brought in nits was perhaps unavoidable, that ration books had to be collected or handed in, and blankets too. What was less comprehensible to me was having to trail round the camp getting appropriate signatures from the many others, such as the electrical stores or transport section, listed on the page-long chit that had to be completed.

What made it worse when I arrived, alone and dispirited, in the depths of Lincolnshire, was that this was only a temporary posting and within a fortnight of 'arriving' at the station I had to go round 'clearing' from it – this time in blizzard conditions. As I struggled and groped my way round, I was almost blinded by the combination of a fine, hard snow that bit into my face like splinters of glass and by the sting of my own tears of useless rage. My spirits were not lifted one evening during my brief stay when, on my way to going on duty, I got a close view of the Lancaster bombers getting ready for take-off. Planes lumbered by me like monsters spitting fire, and the roar of their engines hit me with a new awareness of the contradictions of war. Inside those monsters, I knew, were marvellous young men about to start off on their dangerous mission, but it was one that would bring the same fear and devastation to ordinary, hapless families in Germany as their counterparts in Britain had suffered.

I was able to forget, or set aside, such disturbing feelings when, at the end of the fortnight, I found myself reunited with Maureen, Jess and Jean at another station in Lincolnshire. It was disconcerting, however, to find that many of the Polish airmen based there were as much obsessed with their feelings of enmity against Russia – which for almost three years had been an ally – as against Germany. In fact, the bitterness and desolation of these men was so pervasive that we were not sorry to learn, only two months later, that we were again on the move, even though as a result we were to be split up. I was less content at finding that I was on my way to North Creake, a station in a remote corner of Norfolk, with Jean – whose wheedling manner, although having its uses, often irritated me.

Although the distance we had to travel was not great, it was the end of the afternoon before the slow, stopping train steamed to a halt at Walsingham Station. Neither Jean nor I could make out from the instructions on our travel warrants whether we had to get out at this station or the next one, called Wells-next-the-Sea. After exchanging a few sharp words with Jean, I decided I was going to get off here at Walsingham and Jean, grumbling at my hasty decision, followed. It was the first of many practical matters in which, with her invariable astuteness, Jean was always right – we should have stayed on the train. It did not matter much. The porter at the station phoned through to the camp and all we had to do was wait half an hour for transport to arrive to fetch us, so we sat on our kitbags outside in the sunshine, our tennis-rackets and gas masks piled up beside us.

It was the beginning of May 1944 and, as we were driven away from the station and uphill through green, winding lanes, we could see that the countryside here was pretty, looking and smelling more springlike and less bleak than where we had come from. Next day a priority for us was getting bicycles, and having more or less completed the rest of the 'arriving' process we set off in the afternoon on a ride down the hill to explore what the village of Walsingham had to offer. We discovered that this village we had never heard of before was a place of some importance for religious pilgrimages, and had adapted to tourists. We had tea in a quaint old cottage with leaded windows, where bowls full of marigolds and cowslips on the tables brightened the gloom of low ceilings and heavy beams.

Jean and I quickly settled in to one of the Nissen huts for WAAFs who, as at the other camps we had been at, had a corner of their own in a field on the edge of the site. There was the same mix of girls, the same stove in the middle, the same communal chores to be done, but we were relieved to find the bathrooms and the 'ablutions' were comfortably nearby. We reported for duty and got to know the new team with whom we would now be working. There were two other Met girls, called Pauline and Hilary (the latter a strange girl who kept herself apart), and two forecasters. In the control tower the Met Office on this station was at the back of the block and looked on to a few scrubby bushes, not the airfield. I was disappointed that we would no longer have the panoramic view of the airfield, or of the weather, which had been so dramatic at Woolfox Lodge, especially when there was flying or when thunderstorms and lightning tore open the skies.

We were greeted on our arrival at the Met Office by the senior forecaster, who introduced himself in a well-mannered way as Philip Horne. He was tall and dark, with a strongly cut chin, and he wore spectacles with tortoise-shell-type rims. With his open brown eyes, his face wore a look that was either serious or puzzled. We were to find that he was not so much a serious man as a thoughtful and intelligent one who was more often amused than puzzled, even though his solemn expression often concealed the fact. His assistant forecaster, Desmond, was younger, a boyish creature with reddish hair and a pale skin who was amiable enough but not much interested in either the work or the life on the camp.

At North Creake the aircraft were Stirlings, which looked more old-fashioned and less awesome than the Lancasters I had seen in Lincolnshire, although by today's standards neither was huge. The station was part of Bomber Command, but our aircrews did not carry out bombing missions. It was for some while a mystery to Jean and me what exactly these Stirlings were doing when they went off on their long journeys into the night. In time we found out that their job was to fly in advance of the bombers and drop huge amounts of aluminium strips in an effort to divert German radar before the bombers followed. Probably because the aircraft could keep at a greater height, this was not quite so dangerous as bombing flights, but there were times when aircraft failed to return or limped home damaged and many hours late. One day a pilot who had gone missing several months earlier walked back into the Met Office, but no one could persuade him to say how he had made his way back from enemy-occupied territory.

In a small room behind the Met Office was a rest-room with a bed in it for the duty forecaster's use if he had to stay throughout the night, which was rare. However late operations continued, Philip and his assistant usually preferred to go off to their more comfortable officers' quarters when they ended. As Met girls on shift work we enjoyed many privileges, such as being able to avoid church parades because of our odd hours. Similarly, we could claim rations for our supper while on evening or night duty, which we could cook on a picnic stove in the rest-room, which doubled as a kitchen. Jean very soon managed to get not just rations from the cookhouse, but ration-book coupons that she could use in the shops. With her cajoling charms, she used the coupons to obtain treats for us, such as chops from the butcher's shop at Walsingham. I sometimes popped into the cookhouse for breakfast on my way back to the WAAF site after night duty, but Jean was so pernickety about what she ate that she hardly went there. The NAAFI was more attractive to us, not only for the snacks we could get but also for the company.

Some NAAFIs were good, some bad, and the one at North Creake was good and therefore popular and well used. Within days of our arrival Jean and I had got to know a crowd of electricians, and became part of their circle. One reason why we were made so welcome might have been because as virtual non-smokers we were always willing to swap our cigarette allowance for sweet coupons. Chocolate, for us, was an important part of our diet. In the group were two men, Martin and Patrick, who became our particular friends. Martin was of average height and had gold-blond hair, and always managed to look as if everything he wore was newly pressed. Patrick was also not very tall and had light brown eyes and slightly protruding teeth, which had prompted someone to tell him that he looked like my brother. This became a joke that succeeded in creating a special affection between us. In a comfortably platonic foursome we often went cycling round the country roads exploring the local sights. We also spent many merry hours in the NAAFI arguing about politics – Martin and Patrick liked to tease me about my supposed socialism. Poetry, particularly Shakespeare's, was another topic, because Patrick seemed to regard him as almost an ancestor, having been brought up not far from Stratford-upon-Avon. Martin's first love was music, in which he did his best to encourage our interest. At the time, fond as I became of Martin and Patrick, there was something about both men that struck me as being rather effeminate. It was to be many years later before I realized that this might have been more a matter of class and education (both had been at public schools), the subtleties of which I was still far from adept at assessing – or, less probably, of homosexuality, about which like most young women I knew next to nothing.

Wells-next-the-Sea proved to be as accessible and almost as close as Walsingham, a place where one could go into a café and order egg and chips, or meet friends in the bar of the Crown Hotel or the Globe which looked on to the Buttlands, a pleasant green square with mature trees in the central part of the small coastal town. In off-duty times in fine weather we could cycle out along the causeway by the little harbour and laze in the sun on the sand-dunes and beaches that looked out on to the North Sea.

I thought it was too much sunbathing that brought on the violent sickness which attacked me in the dawn hours one morning in the beginning of June. I had to go into the sick-bay where the medical officer, who had been for many years in the peacetime RAF (and so had little experience of treating women), was inclined to believe I had appendicitis. I managed to persuade him I hadn't, because I didn't want to be sent off to hospital. His junior, who had had more experience of treating women, was not so easy to convince. 'Why have you burnt a mark on your right side with the hot-water bottle if you have no pain there?' he asked. He was rightly resentful when his senior, dismissing his opinion, said he would not send me to hospital if he could help it – and went on to call me soothingly his 'problem WAAF'.

Jean came in to see me and told me that Pilot Officer Wild had been inquiring after me. She was surprised when I looked blank, saying that he was one of the regulars who came into the Met Office for tea or coffee. In a conspiratorial whisper – because Philip had ordered it must not be mentioned outside the office – she reported that there was to be 'something big on tonight'. From these few whispered words I knew that what we had all been expecting was now imminent. Next day, lying there washed out, and with my temperature still wobbling up and down, I could have wept. It was just my bad luck to be in the sick-bay on D-Day, I thought gloomily.

Sick-leave, however, took me back home just in time to catch the start of the second big Blitz on London, this time of V-Is – flying bombs or 'doodlebugs,' as they came to be called. Only a few days following my return to the station after that leave I heard that Gran and Grandad had been bombed out. Mum did not make much of it in her letter, but said that my grandparents had gone to live in Uncle Len's house nearby. Apart from sick-leave all leave had been cancelled because of D-Day, so it was some time before I heard the full story. It was just before five o'clock in morning that the flying bomb had exploded half-way along Lampmead Road. Mum always maintained that she heard and felt the explosion and woke Dad to say, 'You had better get round quick to 49, I can hear your father bellowing.' She probably did, because Gran had been blown – or jumped – out of bed and was hidden underneath it, and it was because he was in a panic at not knowing what had happened to her that Grandad had been shouting. But they had been lucky. Three houses were demolished and six people killed; another twenty-four were seriously injured. In the immediate vicinity thirty other houses were seriously damaged, and in the surrounding area over a hundred more.

My cousin Pete happened to be in London on an Army officer's training course and arrived home before the day was over on compassionate leave. He found that, even though the house was not one of the worst damaged, the blast had shattered the windows and made havoc inside. Gran's prized front room was a shambles: fallen ceilings and plaster, dust and

broken glass covered everything, including pictures and orna-
ments that had been blasted from walls and shelves. Beneath
the bay window Gran's beloved aspidistras lay crushed and
half buried under the fallen Venetian blinds, and the old
carved and mirrored overmantel of polished mahogany lay in
splinters in the fireplace.

By the time Pete got home, the house was empty. Thirty
people from the most damaged houses had to go to a rest centre,
but Dad was there almost immediately to take care of Gran and
Grandad and was very quickly joined by his two brothers –
Len, who had fortunately not yet gone off to work in the City,
and Harold, who was working during the war as a 'special
constable' at the local police station. It was soon decided that
the best thing would be for Gran and Grandad to move in to the
empty top floor of Uncle Len's house in a nearby street. Dad,
given a hand by Harold, took round on his handcart what could
be salvaged from Number 49. It was the end of an era; the
severing of the link with the home Gran and Grandad had
moved into soon after their marriage over fifty years earlier,
where Dad and all their sons had been born and reared, and in
which my brothers, cousins and I had grown up.

It worried me that I should be safe in a remote corner of
England while everyone at home was having to endure so
much. At first I rang home every night to make sure all was
well. As a rule it was Mum who answered the phone and spoke
to me, never Dad, and it was she who told me that the phone
was ringing all day and that Dad hardly knew which way to
turn with so many urgent calls for repairs because of the
damage the bombs were inflicting. But when I got through at
the end of one week of daily calls, Mum said, 'Hold on. Your
dad wants to speak to you.' What he had to say was typically
brief and deceptively curt: 'You don't want to keep ringing up
like this. It's a waste of money.' From Dad this was an order to
stop worrying; and somewhat irrationally, and even though the
air attacks continued relentlessly (with V-2 rockets added to
the doodlebugs), his brief intervention succeeded in relieving
the worst of my anxiety.

One of those who made a point of welcoming me back when I
returned from sick-leave and once more appeared on duty at
the Met Office was the Pilot Officer Wild whom I had not

specially noticed before amongst the numbers of aircrew who crowded in on us. More than six-foot fall and solidly built, with the cuddly look of a teddy bear and thickly waving hair, Adam Wild was a navigator who usually came into the office with his pilot (whose strange nickname was Daisy) and the observer from their crew. On arriving on duty one day to relieve Pauline I found her flirting wildly with the observer, a New Zealander called Billy. Pauline's wide blue eyes in a face of doll-like prettiness belied a shrewd and determined character, and one of the things she was determined to do was to go flying. I thought this was a marvellous idea. It was strictly forbidden to give joy-rides to WAAFs, but this did not trouble us, and, helped by support from Adam and Billy, we managed to persuade Daisy to smuggle us aboard for one of their practice flights.

The Stirling was not the most comfortable introduction one could have to flying, but for me it was a wonderfully exciting one. To see England lying maplike below, to scud along the tops of cloud was, at that time, not an everyday occurrence for anyone other than aircrew. The noise was dreadful and I quickly became quite deaf. This deafness served me well when Adam decided to tease me by getting Daisy to feather two of the four engines. As Adam gleefully pointed to starboard, where the propellers were no longer turning, I wondered what the message was that he was mouthing to me and why he seemed so amused. Not wanting to appear stupid, I nodded my head and smiled back. As he was asking whether I would like to see us flying on only *one* engine, this made me seem pretty cool and much impressed Adam. Thereafter his visits to the Met Office became even more frequent, and soon we were meeting outside more often than in it.

What was left of the summer became idyllic. After D-day, with all leave cancelled, we were thrown more into each other's company than we might otherwise have been. Adam had a small black Ford. We drove around the countryside, got out of it to dally in woods, haystacks or sand-dunes and, parked for hours on the edge of the WAAF site, made love inside it until all hours of the night. Of course, except when on duty, WAAFs were supposed to be in their huts by eleven. But it was always possible to creep in across the fields and so avoid the formal

entrance guarded by the picket hut. There was a good deal of
such coming and going during the night. One girl in our hut
regularly set her alarm for 3.30 a.m. so that she could get up and
go out to meet her love when he returned from 'ops'.

Even for love I should have found it difficult to get up in the
middle of the night, and I knew that after the long, gruelling
night flights Adam was mainly interested in getting to bed as
soon as debriefing was over. But one night while I was on duty
he did come into the office after he had got back, though what
had inspired him to do so I shall never know. It was unexpected
to see him standing there, looking gigantic in his big flying
boots and sheepskin jacket that were merely the outer layer of
numerous others of silk, wool and cotton worn as insulation
against the intense cold endured in the heatless planes. His face
was still icy when he pinned me against the wall and bent his
head down to kiss me. A sublime sensation, a kind of swooning
ecstasy, swept over me. My knees gave way and I should have
slipped down the wall and through his arms on to the floor if he
had not caught me.

I had told Adam all about Andrew, and he told me about the
blonde to whom he had been thinking of getting engaged in his
home town of Birmingham. She was an almost blowzily glam-
orous blonde, he said, but added that she was also a very proper
young woman, and his mother approved of her. Boyish in
temperament, Adam was one of those far from rare people who
pretended that he was not intelligent simply to avoid serious
discussion and who shied away in mock horror from anything
he could label 'intellectual', which was how he very soon
labelled me. (Aspiring intellectual would have been more
accurate.) I think he was as much attracted by me as I was by
him; but he grasped far more quickly than I did that we were
essentially poles apart. Whereas I abandoned myself to our
mutual passion and lived in hope that because of it I might
rouse him intellectually, I came to realize that he felt increasingly threatened by the intensity of both my emotions and
aspirations.

By the end of the year he was doing his best to protect himself
by periodically appearing and disappearing. By the time
Christmas came round I had seen nothing of Adam for more
than a week. I had been quite happy that I was not going on

leave because I thought it was bound to be far lovelier spending it with Adam than at home in London. But Adam had different ideas, and although he did not go home either, he remained out of sight. As I rode round the camp on my bike to go on duty at four o'clock on Christmas Day I was feeling desperate. There was no flying on and the control tower was quiet. When Philip came in to see me on the way to the officers' mess for the evening's festivities I was so glad. He was already in festive mood himself but quick to see how I felt, and knew enough to know why. 'Why are you wasting yourself on that navigator fool?' he said, and then pulled me on to his lap in the office armchair and told me that he had loved me from the day I had walked into the office eight months earlier. I was shocked because I knew that he was married, and I told him primly that he had no right to say such things. But he defended himself vigorously, protesting that his marriage had been finished long before we had met and that he was in process of suing for a divorce. If anything, this news shocked me even more. As a young woman who prided herself on her enlightened views, I believed that divorce was the sensible way to end a bad marriage; and yet the beliefs of those I had sprung from – that marriage, good or bad, was for life – were far more deeply ingrained. But Philip was so obviously a sincere and honour-able man that I could not bring myself to be too harsh on him, and we parted on affectionate terms.

Not long after Philip had left, Jean came in to cheer me up, bringing Josh with her. He was a sergeant engineer in another aircrew. Jean had come back from leave after our arrival at North Creake proudly displaying an engagement ring with a half-hoop of huge white diamonds. She was still wearing it, but I could see she was getting more involved than she had meant to with Josh. When they too had gone, I settled down in the quietness to think about everything. There was some conso-lation in knowing that I was not the only one to be having romantic problems of one kind or another. There was Wyn, a girl in the hut who spent hours putting on heavy make-up and teasing her hair into a high pile on which her cap would hardly fit. She looked like a tart, which was exactly what Jean and I had thought she probably was, especially as she was always out very late at night. We were wrong. It turned out that her problem was whether she should, against her own sense of propriety, be willing to 'go further' with her fellow, who claimed that she should because he wanted to marry her. 'I don't want to end up like Doris,' Wyn announced fiercely as we sat round the stove one evening. (Doris was a girl who had recently been quietly discharged when she was found to be pregnant.) From their letters I knew that Pluckie in Cornwall and Meg in London were just as obsessed by their romantic entanglements as I was by mine. The world seemed to have gone mad. Philip was besotted with me, I was with Adam, and he loved no one – unless it was his mother who, by his own account, was uneasy about this first important rival for his affection. What was the matter with all of us? Pluckie, I thought mournfully, was probably right to believe that unfettered youth added to the upheavals of war made a flammable mixture.

Soon afterwards, Adam and Daisy were posted for retraining to somewhere in Lincolnshire. When they had gone, and convinced that running after Adam would do no good, I made up my mind to relinquish him with as good a grace as possible. But this was easier to think of doing than to put into practice. Lying moping one day in the hut while off duty, I composed a passionate letter in my head to him and then, determined not to write to him, as I had heard nothing from him, I wrote it down in an exercise book. It was the first of many such letters – written but never sent – in which I expressed my longing, frustration and anger. When Adam briefly turned up again, friendly and smiling, but without any apology for the long weeks of silence, I gave him the book of letters to read. Before he went away he gave them back to me. Looking perplexed and rueful, he said gently they were too good to tear up, but that he could not keep them. I took them and tore them up myself.

13

Marion

One good thing that came out of my affair with Adam was my meeting Marion Dunning. She was the matron of the cottage hospital, and a friend as well as colleague of the two general practitioners in Wells-next-the-Sea. One of these, Dr Scott, lived in a pleasant Georgian house that looked out on to the Buttlands and frequently threw his house open to the officers from North Creake. It was here that Marion had met Daisy.

Marion was aged about thirty. She had a long face with a long upper lip, and rather large front teeth. Her hair was her best feature, being abundant and fairish and worn shoulder length. She was not a beautiful woman, or even a pretty one, but her expression was lively and as soon as I saw her I could tell that she was a person of some character. I met her for the first time at the Crown Hotel, which also looked out on to the Buttlands, where Adam had suggested we should meet Marion and Daisy for a drink. I did not warm to Marion at this first meeting, perhaps because, although her views on the position of women in society coincided with mine, her vivacity in expressing them put me a little in the shade. Even so, I did my best to seem friendly, for there was a purpose behind this meeting that was more than just social. I had been telling Adam at some point that I sometimes regretted not having followed one of my ideas for war service, of going into nursing as a VAD, and how I wished I could find some voluntary work of this kind to do in my spare time. While teasing me for my earnestness, and maintaining that all he cared about was enjoyment of life, not doing good to people, I think Adam must have been either touched by my idea or curious to put me to the test. At any rate, it was certainly his idea that he should ask Daisy to ask Marion if she could make use of an occasional volunteer at the cottage hospital.

By the end of the evening Marion and I had agreed that I should cycle down on my next off-duty day to see what she could find for me to do. The cottage hospital was a short distance outside the town, set back from the coast road going west towards King's Lynn. It was a 1930s building which, with its pitched red-tiled roof and small arched porch, looked less like a hospital than a large suburban bungalow. The Marion I had met in the hotel bar, wearing a fur coat and with her hair billowing out, cut a very different figure in matron's uniform. With her starched white head-dress stiffly fanned out on her shoulders and concealing most of her soft fair hair, she looked both impressively dignified and somehow calm and serene. I knew that if I had met her like this as a patient I should have immediately felt that I was in kindly, as well as safe, hands. I had been shown into a small sitting-room to the left of the front door, and it was here that Marion came to greet me warmly. I noticed again her slight Norfolk accent. 'Oh yes,' she said with a wry smile that I was to come to know well, and now deliberately emphasizing the lilt and drag of Norfolk speech, 'I'm "Norfolk" through to my bones.'

Born in a village a few miles inland, where her family still lived, Marion had gone to Norwich to train as a nurse, stayed to work there for several years as a hospital sister, and hardly knew London or anywhere outside Norfolk. After a few minutes' chat, during which we got to know such things about each other, Marion suggested she should show me round. We went first along the short length of the hall, which led to the two wards at the end. Each ward had four beds, but there was only one patient all told because, Marion explained, this happened to be a slack time. I looked at the small operating-theatre and the large kitchen, also off the hall. Apart from the attic bedrooms for the three nurses who, plus some daily help, made up the staff of the tiny hospital, there was little else to see except the garden. This was simply a large grassed patch in which an open-sided sort of summer-house looked out on to the fields. This building was used when needed for tuberculosis patients.

At the end of the short tour, Marion invited me back into the sitting-room which, with the bedroom that led out of it, comprised her private quarters, although she also used the sitting-room for intimate talks with patients' families. Tea appeared as if by magic, brought in by one of the nurses on a tray beautifully laid out, and with fine china and a plate of home-baked scones. All this was very different from the utilitarian conditions of WAAF life in the camp, and spurred my enthusiasm to play a part in this place if I could.

Marion seemed doubtful whether there was much that I could do to help and also puzzled why I should want to. I told her about my interest in nursing, and that I was qualified to do VAD work, but she made clear that being a Met girl sounded to her a far more satisfying way of life than anything she could suggest. Still, she was not averse to my coming again, so I sent home for my VAD outfit and put it on once or twice during subsequent visits to the hospital. But although I was always willing to lend a hand, there seldom seemed much for me to do and before long the purpose of my visits was purely to see Marion. We had become good friends.

Naturally, always a favourite subject between us was the men who had introduced us to each other. I was surprised when I first got to know Marion to find that she was not, as I had supposed, just a friend of Daisy's but in love with him. Much as I liked her, I could not help thinking that to have fallen in love with a man ten years younger was even less sensible than what I had done. Adam was only about a year younger than I was, but I sometimes told myself that part of our problem had been that he was still a boy while I was fully a woman. Yet what had become clear as we exchanged intimacies was that Marion and I were in much the same plight: we were both treated in the same casual way, and both made miserable by it. We had not lost our sense of humour and managed to get a good deal of sardonic amusement from endless discussions on *our* stupidity in pining over men who were treating us so badly, *their* stupidity in not appreciating our obvious qualities – and women's stupidity in general in thinking they could not be happy without men.

Before long I began to spend nights at the hospital. On one occasion I slept in the summer-house in the garden and ate the breakfast that Marion brought out to me, watching the vast sky to the east change from early morning skeins of cream and gold into silvery sunshine. On another night I slept in the men's ward, which was empty. But most often Marion insisted on sleeping upstairs with her nurses and put me in her own ground-floor bedroom, which looked out on to the forecourt and, beyond the road, to the marshland behind the sand-dunes. At night, with the empty countryside all round and just the sea beyond, it felt a bit remote and eerie and so I always made sure I had securely shut the windows before I went to sleep.

Half awake there one morning, I felt something very heavy sitting on the bottom of my bed. Wiggling my feet to move the weight off, I thought at first that it must be Marion's huge black cat, which was called Plod. He was full of character and used to follow her down the road until she reached the crossroads at the edge of town, howl after her until she was out of sight and, however long she was away, wait there for her to return. Then I remembered that I had shut the window before going to bed, and closed the door, so that it could not have been the cat. Startled at this discovery, I opened my eyes, lifted up my head and looked round the room, which was suffused with a rosy glow from the light shining in through the drawn pink curtains. There was nothing on the foot of the bed, no cat, and no one else either.

When Marion came in with a breakfast-tray I told her light-heartedly about this extraordinary sensation that had woken me. To my surprise, her face dropped and she looked dismayed. She said it was a sensation that was only too familiar to her, except that for her it was always a sense of a suffocating weight on her chest that woke her. She confessed that this was why she never minded giving up her room to her guests. It meant she could have a good night's sleep. Try as we did, we could think of no rational explanation, and yet this modern building did not seem to be a likely spot for psychic phenomena, even if one believed in them. Maybe it had more to do with our turbulent emotions than the manifestation of a lost spirit wafting in from the wild North Sea.

I heard a lot about Marion's family, who exasperated her – just as mine did me – and to whom she was quite as deeply attached. Her father was a blacksmith and she had a sister who had gone to university (which was something very special then for a blacksmith's daughter), and two brothers, one of whom still lived in the village and worked with her father. She invited me to stay with her family one weekend, warning me that it would not be much fun because she would have to spend most of the time cleaning. The Dunnings lived in the centre of the village where small cottages were built round a lozenge-shaped green in the shade of gnarled oaks and chestnut trees. In one of the small cottages facing the green lived Marion's brother and his wife and their three flaxen-haired children. Behind their home lay a small courtyard, on one side of which was the tall, timbered and probably Elizabethan house in which Marion had been born and grown up. On the other side of the courtyard was the smithy, where I went across to watch Marion's father at work on the arduous and skilful task of shoeing horses. Each time, it was a small drama to hear the ring of the anvil, see the red sparks flying, and watch the sturdy figures of the men struggling or cajoling the horses into position and then with soothing Norfolk words persuading them to stay there. It was a new experience for me, and yet not one in which I felt strange; it was the world of men's work with which Dad and his yard had made me familiar.

Inside, the cottage was Spartan, except for the parlour which looked out on to the courtyard through windows half filled with ferns. Everything in the house was sparklingly clean. The heavy, dark wood of the furniture had the mirrorlike shine that comes from years of hard polishing. Mrs Dunning was one of those admirable but self-punishing women for whom house-work had become a religion to which, long before arthritis had twisted and bent her, she had become a martyr. This was why Marion had warned me there would be so much cleaning. Her mother would not – could not – lower her standards; but it was only with her daughters' help that she could now manage to maintain them. I naturally wanted to do what I could to help and, after protesting that there was no need, Marion gave me a few things to wash in an enamel bowl which she put on the table in the courtyard. Mrs Dunning limped out and began preparing vegetables, with laborious slowness because of her arthritic hands, while I began to squeeze and rub the things in the bowlful of suds. Then Marion reappeared carrying a bucketful of clean water. She gave her mother an affectionately teasing look as she said, smiling at me, 'You don't need to rub them! Everything we wash here goes in clean! You just have to rinse out the suds!'

I got to know some of Marion's other friends in Wells, most of whom seemed to me to lead astonishingly dramatic lives, not at all like my London-bound ideas of quietly dull rural society. One eminent man in the town, who had had a long-standing love affair with a younger woman for whom he rented a house down by the harbour, was on a constant see-saw of euphoria and despair because of their frequent quarrels which tended to turn into drunken brawls. At such times his lover would threaten to tell his wife or taunt him with how she could ruin his career until, driven beyond endurance, he would turn up in the middle of the night outside Marion's window, noisily drunk and threatening suicide.

Marion's young staff also brought their problems to her, and it was Marion who most often had to advise patients on intimate matters that the doctors felt, being Norfolk born, she knew best how to handle. As with her own family, although she was often exasperated by it, she understood and respected the character of the East Anglian agricultural workers. It was their quirky humour that underlay many of her own self-deprecating stories. 'What can you say', she said one day, 'to a man over forty whose wife has nearly died giving birth to their first child, who claims he did not even know she was pregnant because he "never saw the woman with a needle in 'er 'and", but who looks down at his feet when you try to talk about contraception and will only say, "That won't 'appen agin, Matron. That won't 'appen agin."'

Another friend of Marion's, who lived in a yellow-brick, double-fronted Georgian house facing the Buttlands, was a young woman called Martha. She lived with her parents, both Norfolk people, who took in paying guests, although on a very choosy basis. The drawing-room was elegantly furnished with fine antiques and had a tranquil atmosphere: it looked out on to the green and its trees at one end, and on a conservatory full of green plants at the other. The domestic atmosphere, however, was far from tranquil because Martha's parents carried on a feud that had begun more than twenty years earlier. According to Martha's mother, who spoke about it openly in company, and in front of her husband, she and her husband got on splendidly during their courting days, right up until the morning after their wedding. From then on her husband would speak only in monosyllables to her, and she had never been able to find out why. In spite of this odd domestic relationship, aircrew like Daisy and Adam and other friends of Martha's were always made welcome, and evenings in the drawing-room were always lively and merry. I never worked out whether this much-discussed feud between Martha's parents was real or another expression of Norfolk humour, or of the battle between the sexes that seemed so deeply rooted in Norfolk life.

Where I came from in south-east London the top of the social pile was the Blackheath class – a mass of people who lived in large houses and had superior jobs in schools, the City or the Church. But there was no one identifiable pinnacle in my part of London such as there was in this remote corner of Norfolk which, whether inhabitants of the town protested against it or enjoyed it, lived in the shadow of the Earl of Leicester and his great estate. Radicalism and East Anglian cussedness have a long history of partnership, but many of the townspeople of Wells, I suspect, also had a kind of family pride in their aristocratic landowner. During the war, like everyone else, the Earl was doing his bit. Part of his contribution to the war effort was arranging musical concerts at Holkham Hall for the entertainment of service personnel in the area, such as those at RAF North Creake. As well as being influential patrons, some of the Leicester family had been patients at the cottage hospital, so Marion was amongst the townspeople who received special invitations for such occasions. I was very pleased when she asked me to accompany her to a concert at which Lionel Tertis, the violist, was to perform, because I knew that I would get a better seat than I had on earlier occasions when I had gone as a mere WAAF with Jean.

We arrived in style. Dr Scott and his wife picked us up in their car as they drove past the hospital. On my way to or from North Creake I had often cycled along the beautiful tree-lined avenues that traversed the estate – once, drunk on the scent of the flowering lime trees, I nearly fell off my bike – but I had never before been driven into the forecourt. We alighted to join a small group of other favoured guests in front of the sprawling façade of the yellow stone building which, as big as a palace, looked to me more like army barracks than a stately home. Inside we waited around, as one does, in the main entrance hall. It was impressively monumental with all its stonework and marble, and, eager to get the most out of such grand surroundings, I looked keenly at everything. I caught sight of a message carved in the stone above the doorway which said that this 'seat' had been erected in seventeen something. What a curious place to record something about a seat, I thought; and trying to make sense of it, I decided it must be some kind of ceremonial seat, possibly made of marble. I looked round again, and then turned to Marion. 'Where is this seat?' I asked. She looked mystified, so I pointed upwards at the doorway. The Scotts, who were standing near enough to be listening, looked alarmed. '*This* is it!' Marion said, spreading her arms out to indicate everything. I knew then that I had made a *faux pas* and, because I was embarrassed, I laughed – which fortunately raised the possibility that I might have been joking. I have many times puzzled how it was that I managed to grow up not knowing about aristocratic 'seats' because Grandad (in his Coldstream Guards days as Sir John Somebody's 'officer's servant') had often talked about visits to country nobility. And, after all, he had even told me one day that the unframed oil painting of a Cavalier that had hung over the door in the front room at Lampmead Road was something he had 'picked up' from one such visit.

The Earl's intimate friends and other important guests had chairs at the very front of the hall, whereas others like the doctors, Marion and Martha – privileged retainers, one might say – had chairs upstairs on the balcony that ran round part of the hall. Before the concert began, when the mellifluous tones of Lionel Tertis's viola cast a silent enchantment over all, I had the chance to look out for familiar faces amongst those in air-force blue seated below. I caught Philip's attention, at which he raised his eyebrows and looked quizzical. I smiled, as much to myself as to him, almost fondly remembering that, when we were last on duty together, he had said, 'Cheer up, Phyll. Forget about that twerp Wild and marry me – when I'm free, that is'! Then I saw Martin and Patrick, who made funny faces to show that they were suitably impressed at my superior position. Jean was on duty and could not come; but Pauline, looking from high up more beautifully doll-like than ever, was sitting with Billy. They were holding hands.

Unlike my own romance, and those of so many others I knew about, Pauline's romance with Billy was thriving. Like Adam and Daisy, because of the progress of the war, which by this time was going well for the Allies in Europe, Billy had been posted for retraining somewhere else; but the difference was that he came back as often as he could to see Pauline. They were in love and planning to get married. Between Pauline, Jean and me (and sometimes other trusted friends in our hut) many earnest discussions had taken place about whether Pauline should confess to Billy that she was not a virgin. She had had a short-lived affair with an airman at a previous station who had then left her for someone else. Both Pauline and Billy were Catholics, but Billy was a deeply serious one who accepted and practised the Catholic belief that sex outside marriage was sinful. I was certain that a marriage based on a lie was wrong; Jean was almost as sure that I was right. Pauline agonized, first going one way and then the other. It was months later, after we had all scattered and Pauline was married, that I met her again while we were both on leave in London and found out what had happened. In the end, lacking the courage to tell Billy, she left him in ignorance and hoped he would never know. But his suspicions were aroused on the honeymoon and eventually it had all come out. At first, she said, Billy was devastated; but fortunately his faith, as much as his devotion to Pauline, helped him to accept and forgive. After the war ended, Billy took Pauline to New Zealand, where they settled happily and raised a family.

Almost a year after D-day the horrors of Belsen and the other concentration camps were revealed to the world, and the war in Europe came to an end. North Creake began to wind down. It was a big day on the station with parades and the official departure of the squadron. The Met Office staff were no longer needed and I was among the first to be posted elsewhere.

14

The Aftermath of War

For those at home, although rationing continued and rubble still strewed the streets, the bombings were over. But in some ways the effects of the war seemed to get worse from the time that victory in Europe became surer. For one thing it was as if a great sump had been opened, as more and more servicemen were soaked away to the battlefields elsewhere. Wal went off to India – *en route* to Burma, Malaya and Java; Pete was sent to Greece; and Joe, called up not long before the war ended, was to follow. In among the thousands of others who found themselves packed into the boats going East were Philip and Patrick and Martin, and, although I did not then know it, Adam.

I knew that it would be at least a year before I was demobilized and that I should have to serve out my time on stations which no longer had any real purpose. Soon after I left North Creake the atomic bombs were dropped on Hiroshima and Nagasaki, which brought the war in the East to an end yet ushered in terrifying implications for the future. Struck down again in the following months by the mysterious attacks that had first laid me low around D-day, I fell into a mood of trepidation and gloom. I had recurrent nightmares about death, represented by skeletons and threatening figures in black, and with so many people moving out of my life I felt bereft and uncertain about the future.

During most of my time in the WAAF I had been able to get home frequently, and now, without the attractions (such as the best days at North Creake had offered) to bind me to my new station in the West Country, I began to go home even more often. In spite of the difficulties of travelling throughout the war, it seems astonishing, looking back today, how much time and energy people, including me, spent moving up and down the country so as to keep in touch with those who mattered to them. My own experience of travelling to and from Woolfox Lodge, my first station, was typical of that of hundreds. But there could not have been many service personnel or other war workers who found themselves by the side of the Great North Road, along which hitch-hiking was easy. It was not nearly so easy, for instance, in remote East Anglia; and, although I did hitch-hike home from there on occasions when I had time to spare but could not get a travel pass, I normally travelled from North Creake by train. Typically of the times, this had meant first taking a train on the branch line to Norwich – which sometimes would take two hours to cover the thirty miles! – in order to catch a train to London. Passenger services took second place to the movement of troops or equipment needed for the war effort, so timetables were often disrupted. On one occasion I caught a train to London in the late afternoon, expecting to arrive at Liverpool Street early that evening and to be home at Lee before bedtime. Instead, I spent the whole night in the unheated train, which started and stopped with infuriating uncertainty and pulled into the London terminus at dawn next day. For a journey of a hundred miles, I counted myself lucky to have had a seat and also – as I was travelling with Desmond from the Met Office (who was in fact longing to get home to his fiancée) – to have someone to snuggle up to when trying to doze and keep warm through a very cold night.

Trains were not only always crowded but usually cold as well, but such difficulties did little to deter people who were bent on reunion with loved ones. During one brief leave I made the long journey to Cornwall to see Pluckie, where her landlady had kindly agreed to put me up for a night. On another occasion, Meg got away from her nursing duties and came for an equally brief visit to Wells (where in the digs I found for her the poor girl froze all night, not having enough blankets on the bed). And when my romance with Andrew was thriving, he made light of day trips to Lincolnshire or Norfolk, which meant his spending most of his time on the train, just to see me for an hour or two in the middle.

One thing that continued to work pretty normally throughout the war was the postal service. Thousands upon thousands of letters must have criss-crossed the world from people who in peacetime hardly wrote letters at all, but in wartime such communication became essential for bridging time and space. For me, the long hours on night duty were an excellent time for letter-writing, as well as those idle hours which, like everyone else in the forces, I spent lounging on my bed or round the stove in the hut. One of those to whom I wrote and from whom I received letters most often was Pluckie. A few weeks after I joined the WAAF she had been conscripted into a special part of the Land Army known as the Timber Corps, and subsequently she spent most of her time in Devon and Cornwall. She learnt how to cut down trees, saw logs, make staves and do other forestry work. It was hard work at all times, but cruelly so in winter. Making a cup of tea on freezing mornings deep in the woods meant first of all having to thaw out the bucket of frozen water, while the onset of rain meant arriving home wet through, as well as cold, with no hope of a hot bath in lodgings where conditions were primitive. Most of Pluckie's landladies seemed to expect that, notwithstanding hard days of working in the woods, their Land Army lodgers should help in the house when they were around. Certainly they did not expect them to sit around reading books, of all things. For Pluckie, in spite of her hardships, the beauty of the woods, the West Country and the seasons were at least an inspiration artistically; but she never stopped longing for the intellectual joys of London, amongst which for a while James Elgin was numbered. But in time he too was caught up in the effects of the war, banished by the bank to the provinces to fill gaps that conscription had caused, and lost from view. In the letters that nourished our friendship between the times when we managed to meet, Pluckie wrote about all this, as well as of the books she read, the meetings she attended and the new people she came to meet, and sometimes to love, just as I did to her.

Don was another old friend with whom I managed to keep in touch throughout most of the war, mainly by letters. Increasingly aware that his luck might run out, he remained on 'ops' for the maximum number of tours of duty. Only once, as we were about to part at Charing Cross Station after a meeting, did he speak of his fears. But that was disturbing enough. He had frequent nightmares, he told me, of limping back home with his aircraft, his crew having been shot up and therefore everything depending on him to get back; or, much worse, that he was spiralling down over Germany with his aircraft in flames. It was not long after this that he married a WAAF on his station, and our letters became rarer and then came to an end. Mercifully, his nightmare did not come true and he came through the hazards of bombing attacks unscathed. After the end of the war, so I heard, having a wife and children to support, he had to put aside his writing ambitions for a more secure career as an airline pilot.

With other friends – some new, some old – the end of the war was the prelude to partings, just as the beginning had been. Marion, determined to expand her world beyond Norfolk, soon found herself a job abroad. And promises to write and to keep in touch with her – as with others like Maureen and Tony, or Patrick and Martin, or Philip – were soon eroded by time, distance or diverging interests. In much the same way, as the war years passed, I saw very little of Ben but, as I had become a friend of his family, I received news of his part in heroic actions at sea, and of his happy marriage before the end of the war to a beautiful, curly-haired Wren.

Of course, as well as my friends, there was always the family to see and be seen by, to write to and hear from. When I got home I never needed to be at a loose end while Joe was still around, for he was willing to take me to dances or the pictures or, according to my whim, anywhere else I fancied. Like Joe, Wal, Pete and Ken had their own friends to see when on leave, but they too could be relied on to help me enjoy mine. But because I got home more often, it was my job to keep them in touch with family news, especially when they had all been whisked away overseas. In my 'epistles', as Wal called them, I recounted in lengthy detail all the news from home for which Mum or Grandad could not find time or words – I knew exactly what Pete meant when he said with his gentle smile that the best bit of Grandad's letters was the ending: 'It's always "your loving grandfather, Walter Noble".'

Even though still deeply attached to the family, I was at the same time at the stage of life when my own concerns and interests outside it were to me more important. It was because of this that after Gran and Grandad were bombed out I did not often go round to see them. When I did so, it was no longer as a pleasure but a duty I did not expect to enjoy much; and often the main reason for going, in my own mind, was so that I could give Pete a good account in my next letter to him of how they were getting on. It was an account that, as things got worse, I found it harder to write about truthfully, for I did not want to make Pete sad. In Uncle Len's house Gran and Grandad had two or three rooms on the top floor with a lavatory half a flight down. They lived in the kitchen at the back, just as they had at Lampmead Road, but Gran no longer had a front room she could take pride in (and from which she could at any time peek out on the world of her neighbours passing by outside), and Grandad no longer had his garden to occupy him or in which he could sit out reading his books and papers under the lilacs in fine weather.

On what was to prove my last visit to them – although I could not know it at the time – Grandad launched into a litany of familiar moans, beginning with those about Gran. She was, according to him, becoming more and more absent-minded. He feared that one of these days she would either burn the house down by forgetting to switch off the gas under her cooking, or blow them both up by not lighting it. In spite of his complaints about her, Gran seemed far more like the person she always had been than Grandad did. In fact, she looked to me pretty well. She had always been an indoor sort of person, content to spend most of her time pottering about in the kitchen, and she probably felt less cut off from her former way of life than did poor Grandad. The change that had come over him was far more noticeable. As always, he was sitting in an upright wooden chair with his legs apart, but his trousers were hanging loosely over thinning thighs, his shoulders were sagging and his voice, though still powerful, had a querulous note as he got under way on his next moans, which were about his own health. For years he had grumbled about his bad legs, which were scaly and sometimes ulcerated. But now, he said, the ulcers would not heal up, and, with his softened, piebald hands on which the nails had grown long, he began to unwind greasy bandages to show me just how bad they were. But this was not all. His chest was also bothering him, he said, and the doctor would do nothing to help him.

Distressed by his self-pity, and hoping to distract him, I

began to talk about things to do with the war – subjects in which he had always been keenly interested but which he now brushed aside. Changing tack, I pointed to the mantelpiece, on which there was a large framed photograph in sepia of my cousin Pete as a year-old baby lying on his stomach naked and gurgling. I knew that it used to have pride of place at Number 49 on Gran's kitchen dresser. 'I see that's one thing you saved,' I said. 'I've always thought that was a lovely photo.' Gran beamed. 'It's the most beautiful I have *ever* seen,' she said unusually emphatically and with a hint of smugness – perhaps because she was remembering Pete as the frail, premature babe she had so successfully taken over and reared. I thought of all the other photos of relatives which had been in the old front room but which must either have been destroyed or thrown out when Dad moved things round on his handcart. It would have been tactless to mention them. But I had picked on a good subject because talk of Pete had, for a moment, taken Grandad's mind off his problems. He got up from his chair, reached for the letter on the mantelpiece and fumbled with it. 'Pete has now rejoined his regiment,' he announced slowly and sonorously and, pulling up his shoulders a bit, with a spark of his old military pride.

I could not fail to see and be sad that my grandparents were sinking faster into old age, especially Grandad whose plight seemed far more pitiable because he was aware of, and mourning, his own decline. There was no doubt that the exuberant, and beloved, character I remembered from my childhood was breaking up. Yet I knew that they were fortunate in comparison with many other old people because they were not on their own. Not only were they sharing a house with Uncle Len, Aunt Lil and their daughter, my young cousin Barbara (who often went up to see them and keep them company), but they had their son Harold and his family living next door – and Dad and Mum still not far away and always popping in. But the war had changed everything for them, I thought. It was not a good time to be old, there had been too many shocks and hardships to bear.

For those who were younger, there was the hope and the energy to begin the rebuilding of lives. Nel, for instance, had come back from Colliers End as soon as she could to be rehoused in a council flat not far from the woods where Andrew and I had spent some of our loveliest hours together. It was while I was home on leave, as I stood at the bus-stop waiting for a bus to take me up the hill to visit Nel in her new home, that I saw Andrew one day coming towards me. It was like one of those films in slow motion, as if he were floating slowly closer, rather than walking towards me. By the time he reached me, we had both recovered enough to smile and start talking. He had a day off, he said, and strangely had just run into Dad in the New Tiger, where he had found out that I was home on leave. But the last thing he had expected was to see me! When my bus came along he got on it with me, but jumped off two stops later at the end of his road. He had told me that he was about to be flown across to France to look at the damage – something to do with his war weapons' work. I was envious, of course, and he promised to write to me and tell me about the trip.

I did not tell Nel about the meeting, even when she mentioned in carefully guarded tones that Andrew had continued to keep in touch with her. For one thing, she was naturally more concerned and excited about the turn of events in her own life at this time to worry much about mine. She was delighted to be back in London and impatient for Bern's return from abroad and his demobilization so that they could return to the happy and ordinary family life of which, first as an orphan and then because of the war, she had been deprived.

Andrew kept his promise and wrote of his trip to France, and we saw each other again on my next leave. I found his conversation as intelligent and entertaining as when we had first met. Yet he also spoke with a new tone of bitterness. Unlike Dad, Andrew was not willing to make light of the dreadful time of flying bombs endured by Londoners in the last months of the war. Night after night he had been out on Home Guard duty in the blood and muck of rescue work. With some reason, he believed that he and his comrades had had a much harder time, with far less recognition, than many of those in the regular services.

After an evening out together it was almost as if we had never parted. It was then that I began quite casually to talk about Adam, and what I now believed to be the mainly physical infatuation that had existed between us. As Andrew and I were both acting as if we were more mature and sophisticated people, I assumed that we could talk frankly and openly about the experiences we had each had while apart. Andrew had already mentioned at some point in the conversation a girl at his work whom he was seeing, and I thought that this girl, and perhaps others, must have meant something to him during the many months we had been apart. And perhaps even as much as Adam had meant to me.

I was wrong. By the time I had finished talking Andrew seemed to have shrunk, and his vivid blue eyes which had earlier shone anew with love for me were now full of resentment. I knew then that the talk of the girl at work meant nothing, that he had remained faithful to me and, in spite of everything, had hoped and believed that I would have remained faithful too. Far from being appalled at my mistaken assumption, I felt something like dismay at a devotion that seemed almost un-natural, but I did my best to soothe the wound I could see I had made, and when we said good-night we were again, I thought, happily reunited.

It was another misjudgement on my part: it was weeks before I heard again from Andrew and then only in response to a pleading letter I had sent him. The reply, when it came, was a shock. For too long, he wrote, he had believed me to be what I was not. All the qualities in me that he had so much admired and loved he now saw in a different light. What he had formerly believed to be intelligence and unusual vitality he could now see was mainly a self-promoting vanity. I was superficial and empty, a person whose only outstanding quality was excep-tional self-centredness.

I did not believe that this was a wholly rational assessment of my character, but I feared that there was some truth in it. Of course I wrote back and tried to persuade him that I was not the despicable creature he had described – or if I had been, that I was no longer. On the contrary, I claimed, I had learnt from experience and I was now determined to be as enduringly devoted to him as he had been to me. But at long last Andrew had the good sense to reject a love that had proved so unreliable before and which, had he not rejected it, surely would have proved so again.

15
Coming of Age

It was not Mum's fault at all, but there she was, leaning over me, her brown eyes bright with fear. 'He blames me!' she cried in a high, thin voice. 'He blames me for not calling Dr Carey sooner!'

'Don't take any notice of him,' I said indignantly and, knowing that 'he' was on the other side of the screen, I added for good measure, 'He doesn't know what he's talking about!'

It had begun when I was on my way home on leave and a man on a motor bike stopped to offer me a lift to the station. It was the first time I had ever ridden pillion (and I have never dared do so again). I hated the way it jolted me up and down as we bumped along the road, and bade the kindly West Country-man to put me down as soon as we reached the town and I could see I was within walking distance of the station.

By the time I got home I was feeling ill. The pillion-ride seemed to have started off another of my by now familiar attacks of pain and vomiting. Mum nursed me at home with the cosseting care she reserved for illnesses. As had happened before, after two or three days the sickness and pain subsided. But this time instead of quickly recovering my normal youthful vitality, I felt heavy and tired and continued to lie in bed dozing all day.

'It's not right. You're not well,' Mum said anxiously after a day or two more of preparing food for me that I wouldn't eat.

'Oh, don't fuss,' I complained wearily. 'It's just the same as before. It'll go.' But by the end of the week, knowing I had only two more days leave, I gave in. 'You'll have to call in Dr Carey,' I said grudgingly. 'I may not be well enough to go back on Friday.'

It was tea-time before Dr Carey turned up. It was Edward, of course. During the war it had been impossible to get another doctor to replace Pat after he had been killed in the Blitz, and although the war had been over for several months, it was too soon for anything to have changed. We had to wait all day before we heard his imperious ring at the doorbell. His peremptory 'Where is she?' cut short Mum's anxious explanation, and he was up the stairs and standing beside me in a moment. He looked tired, harassed and old; the demands of the war years in London had taken a heavy toll on him. His manner was as rushed as ever as he asked in his thick brogue that a lifetime in south-east London had left untouched, 'Now what's t'matter wid you?' Before I could answer he went on, 'Let me look at yer' – and it was only then that I noticed the change which had come over me. Alarmed, I saw that my normally trim, flat abdomen had become unbelievably swollen and hard. Even more alarming, it was obvious that Edward was as concerned as I was, and almost as agitated as Mum. 'Have yer got a telephone here?' he asked, and rushed down the stairs after her to call an ambulance.

Behind the screens at the hospital an hour or so later Mum's cry – 'He blames me!' – was hardly more eloquent than her anguished eyes. I had no more pain, but my nose was now blocked as if I had a cold, and mere breathing had become an effort. At the same time, apart from my concern about Mum, I felt sort of cocooned and peaceful. Well, I thought with an inward sigh at the effort I'd got to make, one thing's clear – I can't just die and leave her for ever blaming herself.

Mum had disappeared. Unbeknown to me, the doctor who had examined me had also given her the grim message that it was likely I was not going to survive, so she should hurry back home and get her husband. She rushed out of the hospital to catch a bus to take her the two miles to Lee. In her panic, she forgot that we now had a telephone and that she could have rung Dad to tell him to come and join her at the hospital.

Two hours later I was on my way to the operating-theatre. I was feeling brighter and my breathing had improved after an hour on a saline drip. Mum was no longer in my mind, my thoughts had wandered away to all the happier times I had enjoyed before everything seemed to go wrong. If I were going to die, which of the young men who for a while had loved me would care now? I wondered wearily. And which of them did I really care about anyway? Ben, Don, Kit, Andrew, Stephen and Adam, and perhaps Philip too – I had surely cared a bit for all of them for a time, but did I really love any of them any longer? Maybe, I thought wryly, I shall find out, at last, when I come round calling for someone after the op.

I could not help noticing that the doctor who had so upset Mum and who was getting ready to operate on me was a most attractive man. He exuded authority, had fine dark eyes, thick dark hair, and a charming Central European accent. Most impressive of all, he bore a striking resemblance to James Mason, one of my favourite film stars. His name was Pollitzer, and his background, I was later to discover, was as romantic as his appearance: he had escaped to England when the Germans invaded Czechoslovakia.

I was still conscious when I was wheeled into the operating-theatre. Under the bright lights, where Mr Pollitzer stood dressed in a snowy-white garb and looking even more like James Mason, the impression of film fantasy intensified. However, when I looked up into the very blue eyes of the anaesthetist as his masked face came close, I knew with a pang of fear that this was no fantasy. 'Breathe in steadily,' the anaesthetist said, and then there were just voices swirling somewhere mistily. I wanted to cry out 'Don't start yet!' but, before I could do so, oblivion enfolded me.

Aeons later, as I floated upwards infinitely slowly from a kind of bottomless well, I heard my own voice coming from somewhere above or outside of me. And then everything came together and I felt myself smiling; for that disembodied voice, which was mine, was not calling for Ben or Kit or Don or Andrew or Philip, or even Adam. It was calling 'Mummy'! A moment later, roused by other voices, I opened my eyes.

'Don't make a noise, dear,' said one of the nurses leaning over me. 'You're all right. You're back in the ward.'

I did not feel all right. For days I floated in and out of consciousness and time stood still. In spite of the bottles of blood or plasma that were being dripped into me, it was as if every cell in my body had been drained empty. To speak in the merest whisper or to turn my head was like climbing a mountain. Immobilized by weakness and things attached to me, I longed for the visits of Pollitzer who, in my fantasies, became the God I could not believe in, and on whose hands I felt I depended for some kind of life-giving current of the strength I so desperately needed.

In reality, of course, it needed more than faith in Pollitzer's touch to pull me through, because what I was suffering from was a rampantly generalized peritonitis, which demanded drastic treatment. (So much for being a 'problem WAAF' on D-day.) I held on to life. A fortnight later, cheered up by my apparent recovery, Mum was pleased to bump into Pollitzer in the corridor on her way homewards. 'She's much better, Doctor, isn't she?' she said.

To her dismay he replied, 'She has youth on her side, and she is fighting with us. But do not raise your hopes too high.'

Everyone was amazed that I had survived so far. People in white coats arrived at the bottom of my bed intent only, it seemed, in marvelling at my being there at all. One consultant declared, 'The hospital ought to put you on display at the front entrance.' I felt almost proud of myself, and a week or two later was boasting that I intended to be out of the hospital in three weeks' time. But it was six weeks before I was allowed out of bed, and six months before I returned home again. For much of that six months I was in fact in a terrible mess. Twice a day, when the wound was dressed, the staff wore masks and lit incense because of the shamefully foul-smelling pus that was flowing out of me. Propped up by half a dozen pillows and able to move only my head and one unsplintered arm, I was struck with horror and fear when – before Pollitzer could stop me with his sharp command, 'Don't look down!' – I saw the gaping, oozing wound that looked like three giant open mouths in my abdomen.

The nights were the worst, and interminably long. On most nights it was the same middle-aged, diminutive and fierce nurse who arrived at my bedside to see to my needs. With her dark hair pulled back in a tight, old-fashioned bun under her small starched cap, she would lean over me venomously. If I needed a bedpan she would disappear again for what seemed hours to get someone to help her to lift me. The someone was always, and incongruously, her identical twin sister. It was as if they had appeared from a Grimm's fairy-tale. One each side of the bed, these diminutive figures would heave me up and on to a bedpan that was always as cold as ice – and then of course leave me for so long that my buttocks grew numb. By choice, they worked only at nights, and I never heard them speak gently or kindly to anyone. Far from being angels of mercy, one had the feeling that the main satisfaction of this ghoulish pair was not tending the sick, but disposing of the dying. I did not feel safe in their care.

While I was recovering in the hospital there were several deaths, and always at night. There was the wizened old woman who had come in with a fractured thigh and who took all of one night to die. She lay behind screens in the bed opposite mine. It was not long after the ward had settled down for the night that she began to call again and again for someone named Willy. Her voice had at first the high-pitched tone which from my childhood I remembered mothers had used when a child had not come home before dark. Had she, I wondered, returned in her delirium to the time when she had been a young mother wandering round the local streets looking for her son? If it was her son, he was not at the bedside. I wondered if Willy had been an only child who was killed in the First World War, for no one at all had come to visit the old woman. As the hours slowly passed, the cry took on a keening note, but it was always the same name called over and over again: 'Will-EE. WILL-ee'. The first call was expectant, the second a little exasperated. When at last the calling stopped a communal, rustling sigh of relief swept through the ward. But the horror of the night was not over. There was the breathing which followed. Time dragged as the ward listened in mesmerized, oppressive fearfulness to the dreadful, raucous sound of the old woman struggling with death. It was dawn when, to everyone's relief, it ended and the odious twins bustled about noisily laying out the corpse and stripping the bed.

I was not relieved, and far sadder, when Mrs Green died. She was in the next bed to mine. In the early days, when I could only with difficulty speak in a whisper, she was always listening and looking out for my needs. She was a widow with a daughter of my age who visited her often, so that I became friendly with both of them. But as I steadily got better, Mrs Green slowly declined, and one day I learnt from her daughter that she had an inoperable cancer. This sweet-natured, gentle woman from Bermondsey had struggled through difficult years as a widow to give her daughter a better chance in life than she herself had had. She put up with the pain of her illness with the same stoicism no doubt with which she had faced her hard life.

'Why should you suffer like this when you're so good?' I asked angrily one day, overcome by the unfairness of it all.

'I don't know, but it's not for us to judge,' she said mildly. 'You're like Rose. It's because you're young.'

She died one night as quietly and unprotestingly as she had lived.

In spite of the pain, and the dying, and a sister whose dedication and superb nursing skill did not stop her from bullying patients who 'fussed', and reducing to tears almost daily the younger nurses who did not come up to her high standards – in spite of all this, and mainly because of Lennie, there was plenty of laughter as well as sadness in the ward. Lennie came from Poplar, where the docks had suffered heavily from the bombing about which she, as an air-raid warden, had a mixture of horrid and humorous stories to tell. At weekends she held court round her bed to a large circle of friends and relatives, but not her husband who was still serving overseas. She was in her thirties, although she looked older, a scrawny blonde with a strong Cockney accent and the gravelly voice of a heavy smoker. A lung complaint had brought her in, and from behind the screens placed round her bed Lennie could some-times be heard not so much crying out as hollering and swearing. But mostly she was the ward's comic. She was of course forbidden to smoke, yet she usually had a cigarette dangling from her mouth as she wandered about spreading good cheer with her banter. Her language was fearful – 'bleed-ing' was her favourite expletive – but she was so patently good-natured, kind and brave that she was one of the privileged in whom even Sister could see no wrong.

The hospital was one of those set up to meet the demands of war – and so, as it was to turn out, one of the pioneers in the National Health Service that was to follow it. As it was an 'emergency hospital', the wards consisted simply of half a dozen long, prefabricated huts put up in the grounds of a large house (which served as the admission and administrative block). But the grounds were beautiful, with mature trees, shrubs and walkways; and on the day Sister turned my bed to the window so that I could see the first pale, pointed buds of rhododendrons breaking out it was, as we both knew, a symbolic moment.

By then I had become absorbed into the pattern of life in the ward, in which the high spots of the day were the visit from Pollitzer in the morning and the arrival of friends and relatives in the afternoons or evenings. Mum, of course, came almost daily, facing my petulant demands with extraordinary patience. Dad did not so much 'visit' as come to see with his own eyes that I really was still there. He never sat down, and within a minute of arriving would have to take a walk round the grounds to escape either from the wards or his repressed emotions.

It was during one of Dad's walkabouts that Mum, in a matter-of-fact voice, as if it were one of the most natural things in the world (which indeed it was), told me Gran and Grandad had both recently died. Grandad had gone first. Even though it was summer, his bronchitis had returned. Dr Edward had been called, but there was nothing he could do. 'Don't forget he was eighty-four. It was really old age, you see,' she said. Then a few weeks later Gran had fallen down, fractured a thigh-bone and been sent to Lewisham Hospital. I remembered my last visit to them both, and how miserable it had been, so I found it easy to agree with Mum that it was all for the best. By the time Dad came back we were talking about something else. I did not even trouble to see if he looked sad, as he must have been.

After they had gone I thought most about poor Gran, sparrowlike and vague, who unlike Grandad had died in hospital. I knew she would have been distressed and even more confused than usual without Grandad because, despite all his moaning about her, he really cared for her and she had depended on him, as he did on her. To think of her dying in the ward, perhaps as slowly and painfully as the old lady whose death we had witnessed, was even more disturbing for me. Mum was right, I decided. It was best not to dwell on it. And so, carelessly, I shoved Gran and Grandad into the past and returned with relief to the present – which was who would be coming to visit me this evening.

There would be no lover, that I knew; and with brothers and cousins and most of my friends, either far from London or overseas, I should have felt pretty much bereft had it not been for Meg. Jean, it is true, when on leave had come once or twice (full of her plans to get married as soon as her fiancé returned from overseas). But I had seen nothing of Pluckie. She rang Mum from time to time to find out how I was, and wrote to me, but she had not come to see me. I knew that she had left the Land Army almost as soon as the war ended, and that she had gone to a teacher training college. She was taking one of the post-war emergency courses set up to make good the shortage of teachers following the hostilities. Serious and conscientious as ever, Pluckie was for the time being wholly immersed in her own affairs.

Fortunately for me, Meg was still slogging away as a VAD at the Royal Herbert Hospital in Woolwich, which was not far away. My long stay in hospital in a ward with a disciplinarian as sister had given me a clear picture of just how far removed from the reality my early fantasies of nursing had been. I had come to understand the pettifogging treatment and unending drudgery that junior nursing staff had to endure, which I had not done from my experience as a trainee VAD under gentle Staff Nurse White at St John's Hospital, or from my links with Marion and the cottage hospital in Norfolk. I knew that Meg too had been reduced to tears by her ward sister, and often felt almost unbearably ground down, until she found a more sympathetic environment in which to spend her off-duty hours.

In a corner of the Royal Herbert Hospital the Army Education Corps had set up, mainly for the benefit of its long-term patients, what had seemed to me, when I was smuggled in one day to visit it, a kind of mini-Morley College. It had inevitably become the focal point for the intelligentsia – staff or patients – within the hospital precincts. There Meg had met Jake, a tall young man with auburn hair, fine features and a narrow-eyed, feline beauty, whose intellectual arrogance was tempered by a rare amalgam of personal modesty and brilliant wit. What added to his many charms was the fact that, although he was totally opposed to war, he had been dropped into France on D-day carrying, as an RAMC medical orderly, stretchers in place of arms. Once or twice a week, for month after month,

Meg brought Jake along to entertain me. They would sit by my bed, Meg looking charming in her neat, navy blue uniform with its moplike cap, and Jake in khaki. Apart from the Pollitzer-magic, it was the best treatment I could have had.

There was plenty for us to talk about. For one thing there was the new Labour Government which we, voting for the first time, felt we had helped to bring into being. Then there were all the exciting post-war plans for education, health and social security that Meg and I would argue (with Jake always more sceptical) must surely do away with many of the injustices which had roused our indignation in the past. Above all, of course, we were interested in discussing where our own future lay, and how we could avoid being trapped once again in the boring office jobs from which the war had released us. Jake's friends in the Education Corps were urging him to try for a place at Oxford University, and Meg was thinking about training for some kind of career in social welfare. Under the schemes for the resettlement of service personnel these were all realistic ambitions. I was certain of only two things: that I was not going back to the bank, and that I had to find 'something worthwhile'. I had almost died and was very lucky to be alive, so it seemed to me as if I had been given a second life for which I had some kind of debt to repay. I realized that the war that had brought disaster and tragedy to millions had for me been mainly a happy voyage of discovery. At the beginning of it I had been a naïve and innocent teenager, as much in love with myself as with life. It had been easy then to scorn the idea of marriage as lightly as I had Dad's jibes that, going on as I did, I should end up a spinster. At twenty-four, no longer innocent, still unmarried, I was less sure that somehow, somewhere there must be a better future ahead for me. If there were, I knew that I must take a different path to find it.

It had been spring when I first went into the hospital, and by the time I left the leaves on the trees were turning gold. When we got home Mum fussed round me, urging me to sit in Dad's chair by the fire while she got me tea. I knew that I looked skeleton thin – I had lost several stone in weight, and in her eyes I was still an invalid. At some time I should have to go back to the WAAF, even if only to get demobbed. But if Mum had her way, my return would be delayed as long as possible, if not somehow avoided altogether.

While Mum was in the kitchen I looked round the living-room. After the months in the ward it seemed strange and yet as if time had slipped back, as if I had never left home, as if I were once more a child. I began to weep, and then to sob.

Mum rushed in from the kitchen. 'Whatever is the matter?' she cried, sounding almost as distressed as I was.

'I don't know!' I said.

'But what's *wrong*?' she pleaded, tears beginning to stream down her face too. 'Are you in pain? Aren't you glad to be home?'

I could not explain. I *was* glad to be home, or at any rate relieved – and yet I felt as if I were grieving bitterly. But what for? The mistakes of the past? A new sense of my own vulner-ability, and of the irrecoverable losses that I now knew were part of life? The end of youth – or at least of the girl I had been?

'I'll be all right in a minute,' I said to Mum, touched by the melting, soft brown eyes, and with a new sense of gratitude. After all, it was her love and this home that would sustain me until I was strong enough to set off again in pursuit of my own nebulous star.